T0194189

From Catalina... with Love

Doris Pereyra-Rosenberg

authorHOUSE®

AuthorHouse™
1663 Liberty Drive
Bloomington, IN 47403
www.authorhouse.com
Phone: 1 (800) 839-8640

Published by AuthorHouse 02/14/2020

ISBN: 978-1-7283-4702-8 (sc)
ISBN: 978-1-7283-4701-1 (e)

Print information available on the last page.

Any people depicted in stock imagery provided by Getty Images are models,
and such images are being used for illustrative purposes only.
Certain stock imagery © Getty Images.

This book is printed on acid-free paper.

Edited by
Karen Rosenberg

Jacket Design, Text Formatting
& Additional Editing
by Thomas Porky McDonald

Back Cover artwork by Julio Candelario.
Front Cover photo, Author Photo, Covers Background photo
and all Inside Images from the Author's Collection.

I dedicate this book to
my grandchildren:

Dorian

Justice

Noah

Juniper

Eric

Lila

Maya

I love you all so dearly.
I thank all of my children for giving me
the opportunity to be in my grandchildren's lives.

**Long ago, I read some words that
I want to share with you:**

"I want to surround myself with people
that know how to touch the heart."

"People that dance, sing, laugh and love adventures."

"People to whom life's struggles taught them
to grow with gentle touches in their soul and
continue to believe in love and goodness."

Contents

(I)

The Home of My Father
(La Casa Paterna)

(I)

The Home of My Father
(La Casa Paterna)

My memories of that day are like shadows. I sit on a low wooden bench in our house. It's a big wooden house, with many rooms. People walk slowly around me. People without faces or names, lots of sad people, walking and talking in low voices. Someone stops to pat my head. Someone picks me up and sits me on their lap and talks to me. Someone takes my small hand in theirs and moves around, from room to room. Each room is crowded with other sad, quiet people. There was the main bedroom, my parents' room. No one took me there. People were loud there. Crying hard and banging on the door. But no one dared open it.

I couldn't find my mother or father. I couldn't find my brothers or sisters. Where were they? Were other people sitting them on their laps, stroking their hair, whispering into their ears? Mario, Esperanza, and Manases were older than me, so they probably knew what was happening. And Felicia was just a baby. This day, this day that weighs so heavily on me all these decades later. Amongst my siblings, we have never spoken about it. Yet I am sure this is the day our lives cracked open in such a terrible way. The day our papa died.

The day we lost my father is the day my memories begin. I was three years old. My father was 33.

My memories continue in their strange, shadowy way. Some shadows have more shading than others, some are steely gray. Mario, Esperanza, Manases, and Felicia fall into the grey then — I cannot even make out their outlines. Even Mama doesn't emerge from the grey. I cannot see, smell, or feel her as a young woman.

Things come into focus at the river behind our house. We'd fetch water for drinking and bathing. We'd walk out the back door and down the narrow path. The path was alive with wildflowers growing on both sides, blues deeper than the sky, pinks and reds that made me want to giggle. I loved that little path. The river was a different story: I was attracted to it and terrified of it at the same time. It looked and sounded so friendly but I feared entering it alone. I was afraid of whatever could be underneath.

Whenever it rained hard, the river swelled and the water churned brown. I loved sitting there and looking at the big brown river snake slowly downstream. I felt peaceful there, watching it. When I was tired of crying, I would walk down the narrow path to the river. I'd lie down in the green and refreshing bushes and fall asleep. After a while, I'd wake up listening to the sound of the water, melodious and peaceful, as it flowed downstream. Whenever my siblings were looking for me, they knew where to find me. I went there also when I ran from my mother after stealing sugar from her little container hanging high up above the stove.

I loved the river but I hated fetching water for the house. I tried to balance the wooden container on my head but it was *so heavy.* At night, we all shared the same container and the same water to wash our faces and our feet. I hope we all did our faces before our feet!

When the river flooded, the sweet water fish were abundant. My older brother Mario would take me to fish so we could feed our family. With him, I wasn't afraid. He was a skinny but strong boy. I trusted that he could protect me from the river's current. I'd hold onto the pockets of his khaki shorts and together we'd struggle upstream. But it was pleasant. When the river was furious like this, because of all the rain water, the shrimp bobbed everywhere around us. Even I was able to catch some with my bare hands.

Mario also went under the rocks to look for crabs. This I didn't do. The crabs were angry and could bite you. But Mario had a technique. This was important because it meant we would have a very good dinner that evening.

When we returned from the river, we'd make a fire behind the house using dry wood and dry grass, and some large rocks. We'd roast our catch. It was a feast. Fresh river food and the smell of the roasting was *so delicious*. I remember sitting in a circle with everyone, but I cannot see any of their faces: not Felix or Mario or Esperanza or Felicia or my mother.

I don't remember our mother ever joining us.

Maybe she was inside the sad house just crying for my father. He was her only love, I think. When she wasn't angry with us, or screaming at me, or singing sad songs, or just crying in a corner, she would just sit there and look at us, like she could see through us. Poor woman: she was probably trying to decide what to do with this bunch of children. She was young and lonely and angry. She was 28 years old with five children between 3 months and 9 years old.

After Papa left we stayed together for a while.

We used to sleep 2 or 3 to a bed. Our beds were made of strong black wood with 4 large poles, one on each side. The mattress was made out of dry leaves mixed with cotton balls, placed inside a large rough fabric. We dragged the mattress outside every morning, under the sun, because some of the younger ones would pee in bed every night. So our mattress smelled like pee, but we didn't mind.

When an uncle or cousin would visit, Mama would put that man or boy in bed with us. I hated this because during the night, I would feel something hard touching my little body. (Today I can understand). But I never said anything to anyone. Why? Maybe I thought it was normal. Also, at the time, I couldn't name the hard thing. A fist? That's how it felt.

I also remember that my private parts itched like crazy, like they were on fire. I imagine this was due to our lack of hygiene. The outdoor latrine was very old and run down. We used leaves from the trees as tissue to clean ourselves. Sometimes the boys cleaned themselves by rubbing up against the poles on the wall.

I guess that was the main reason we had so many worms in our bellies. We were pale and skinny with big bellies. I imagine these worms ate whatever nutrients we got. When the worms got really bad, Mama would take leaves and make a bitter, smelly drink for us. She'd give it to us first thing in the morning, with our stomachs empty, so that the worms would be hungry waiting for something to eat. They despised that drink as much as we did. We'd sit on the *bacinilla* (portable toilet) and watch dozens of white, long worms come out of our behinds. I cried as soon as I saw one coming out. I'd jump up from the *bacinilla* and start running away. But strong arms brought me back and I had to sit there until all of the worms slithered out. This memory just doesn't fade. Today, whenever it rains and I walk outside, I won't look down. I hate to see the little worms that crawl out of the dirt in the rain.

As an adult, and as a mother myself, I try to understand my mother, and her behavior towards us. I need to understand in order not to judge.

She found her true love and they had 8 children. She buried him when she was 28. She buried three of her sons around this time too: Julio Cesar, Efrain, and Radame. I don't remember the baby boys at all, only their names.

My shadow of a memory of that house is shrouded in sadness. Sadness lived inside. Outside was a different world. Our house was built on an elevated piece of land. From a side window, I could see the sweep of the whole valley. I could see cows and horses, tiny in the distance. Closer by I'd see chickens, ducks, and so many other kinds of birds, whose names escape me now.

The house was big and made of unfinished, rough wood. It was built on top of some high, strong rocks. These rocks formed the foundation. We could go under the house and play. That became our playground. We didn't have conventional toys. But we made up our own. We made dolls out of corn. We made cows and horses out of mangoes and little people out of sticks and leaves. Sometimes a neighbor's chicken would come over and mess up our things. Sometimes the cats would bat around our toys with their paws. Sometimes the pigs rolled around down there.

I played with my brothers and sisters but I cannot see their faces or hear their voices.

A huge kitchen stood out from the side of the house. It had a home-made stove built out of dirt and something else—I don't remember what. Mama cooked our food using wood and dried grass for fuel. It got so smoky that our eyes watered whenever she cooked. The kitchen was big enough for all of us to sit in (on the floor). I remember sitting on the floor, pressed close to other little bodies, hungry and waiting for some concoction from my mother. Like hot chocolate. It smelled *soooo good*. I also remember the smell of fresh cooked *gandules*, and coconut candy. This coconut candy smelled best of all. After she spooned out the candy, she'd let us each run a finger along the side of the pot, scraping out the leftover caramelized coconut. The candy she spooned out she sold or traded at the *purperia* (*bodega*). So we really savored what we could finger out from the pot.

This large kitchen had a window and a high shelf where we washed the dishes. I remember climbing up an improvised step to reach the shelf, so I could wash dishes. We took turns. Though I didn't like scrubbing the pots and plates, I loved the view. I could look down over the valley and out to the ocean. I loved looking out at the sea.

Fruit and nut trees surrounded the house. I remember the almond tree, with enormous, graceful branches. And the beach grape tree, heavy with sugary red fruits. A few paces down the path stood the lime tree. Behind the house a coconut tree spread its wide branches. Many days the only food we ate came from those trees.

And the flowers! I remember the gorgeous gardenia tree, with big white flowers that released their aroma each evening. I adored that tree. When I was grown, my mother told me that the gardenia was my father's favorite.

We also made use of our towering *higuera* tree. The large round fruits were not edible, so we'd scoop out the flesh and dry the sturdy shells in the sun. Then we'd use the dried shells as dishes, as vessels for fetching river water, and as salt and sugar containers. And when the higuera shells were fresh and tiny, Mama would place them on the fire, squeeze the liquid out and apply them to our ears for earache.

I liked to sit alone in front of the house, inside the tall grasses, where no one could see me. I'd stare at the sea, shimmering in the far-away distance. I sat in peace in my hiding place. That is one of my strongest visions, even today.

It is painful for me to talk about this. My intention in mentioning all of this is to say to all the young parents to be so extra careful with your kids. Do not leave them alone with other people when they are very young. This is another sad episode from that distant past. It is crystal clear in my mind. I was four or five years old. There was a family member, a man. I still feel his smell. I was left alone with him. Many times. I have no idea why we were left alone. I have no idea where everyone else could have been. He would get on his knees in front of me and would touch my genitals with his member. I don't remember physical pain, so maybe he just touched the outside of my genitals. Each time he ejaculated. I didn't know what he was doing. But I only knew that I didn't like that smell. The smell was so strong. I hated this smell.

I try to imagine how I felt at that time, but I can't. I just remember that figure in front of me and the stench. One summer day, about 62 years later, already a grandmother, the mailman rang the bell to deliver a package to our apartment. When I opened the door, my stomach froze. I smelled the man in front of me when I was a child. This was the one and only time this happened.

I will never mention his name because it would only bring pain to family members that I love. The honest truth is that I don't hold anger or resentment against him. He was just an ignorant young man. I don't think that he tried to hurt me. I prefer to think he was satisfying an animal instinct, without knowledge of the damage he caused.

For the first couple of years after Papa died, Mama tried to support all of us. She worked washing clothes in the river. She picked cacao. When she picked cacao, the landowners paid her in cacao. Mama would dry the cacao behind the house and used some to make hot chocolate for us. The rest she'd trade at the *pulperia*. The drying cacao seeds released a sweet, fruity smell. Mama also picked fresh peanuts and set them out to dry. We'd sneak outside and gobble up the peanuts before they were dry. Mama yelled at us for doing this. But we were hungry.

One day Estanislao Martinez arrived. Though he was Mama's father, he hadn't shown her much care when she was growing up or after she became a widow. Many years later she told me that he came to her because he was old and needed a place to live. She wasn't happy about this, but she let him stay.

One more mouth to feed.

Shortly after he came to live with us, other things started happening. A young farmer came to visit Mama. He was married, with lots of children. He owned a lot of cows and other animals, and produced cheese and milk for market.

Well, every time Mama's farmer "friend" came to visit, we were happy. He brought fresh cheese and eggs, enough for all of us. Then one day there was a new baby in the house. My mother had this young farmer's baby. I'm sure Mama was mortified by this situation, but what could she do? She called her new baby Rafael. To us, it was life as usual, I imagine. I don't remember any drama whatsoever. In fact, the farmer gave my mother a cow. That was a bonanza. Every morning we could drink warm milk from that cow. She was black and white and so gentle. We were never afraid of her.

Mama pressed her father into service. His job was to care for this cow and to get the milk every morning. I remember standing next to him while he milked the cow. I stood there, holding a jar. I put this little jar under the cow's belly, and it would fill up with bubbling white liquid. It was *sooooo good*. But our family continued to grow. There came another baby boy. Now Mama had two extra mouths to feed. Then the farmer stopped visiting. Maybe his wife found out. Maybe he didn't want to have more kids or give away more cows. We never saw this farmer again, but now we had a cow and two more brothers.

Mama would send us far away on errands. When it rained, I didn't want to go. It got so muddy and worms crawled out of the wet soil. None of us owned shoes. To cover our heads, we'd cut large leaves from plantain trees. At least we didn't go hungry on those trips. We'd sneak onto farms and steal mangoes, oranges, and bananas. But we'd have to avoid the farm animals: the dogs, cows, horses, and mules. The cows on those farms were the worst—they could be vicious. We'd distract them and work fast. Mario would scamper up the trees and throw the fruit down to us. I became a good catcher. Whatever we couldn't eat we'd bring home to Mama. Ah, we also had amazing luck picking fresh corn. We'd come home with our little skirts and pockets full of corn.

I remember doing these things with my siblings but I cannot remember their faces.

In those years I suffered from whipworm disease. I was told that these parasites attached themselves to the bowels and fed on their host's blood. One time I was at the outdoor latrine and part of my intestine came out. I screamed and ran out. My mother and Mama Mecha, a very good and dear aunt (the wife of an uncle), took a warm cloth and placed it on my rectum until the intestine went back inside. I think that poor children in these remote areas survive because of some super-power design. The water we drank was contaminated. The water from my lovely river. I remember fetching water near where the cows and horses bathed.

Even though we went hungry, even though people didn't hug us, or sing to us, or soothe us, we were happy. It's a feeling – no, a memory – that we were happy, because we were all together: doing errands together, sleeping together, and sharing our miseries together.

I think and wish to believe it so.

That was just us kids. Mama was a different story. She was always working. And she was always angry. Once she tried to hang me from one of the beams in living room. My brother Mario untied me. Several times she took me to the river (yes, my lovely river again) and forced my head underwater. She did it so I would stop crying. I cried a lot. I'd cry, cough, pee, and vomit—all at the same time. Maybe she thought dunking my head in the river was the only way to quiet me. I had no choice: either I could stop crying or my lungs would fill with water.

Why did I cry all the time? I really don't know. Maybe I missed my papa. Maybe I missed when he'd hold me or sing to us. I don't remember the songs but I remember his tender voice filling the house. After he died my mother was too angry and worried to be soft with us. Imagine, seven little bodies looking for more than she could give.

We went to a small rural school. The school was in a large and dilapidated wooden house, with 5 or 6 rooms. Every morning we'd stand in line and sing the Dominican National Anthem and salute the flag. We had to wear uniforms made out of a soft brown fabric. These are the only memories I have about this small country school.

But I do remember the long walk to get there. One day I was walking by myself and I got lost. I was surrounded by cacao trees and their branches looked like sinister arms and heads. I started to cry. I called for my grandmother who lived around there. At first I cried softly, but as I kept on turning and not finding a path, my cries became louder and louder. Mama Cora, Mama Cora, I cried. (She was my father's mother).

Mama Cora was okay. A little wild in her personal life, but shy with us, yet harmless. I don't think she cared much about us because I never saw her visit us. She was a beautiful, tall and slender woman. She lived by herself in this remote area. I don't understand how she could live there and not be afraid. There weren't any houses around, just cacao trees. I don't know how she supported herself. Maybe she had a boyfriend that helped her, I guess.

I finally reached her house. I have no idea how I got there. Mama Cora asked me if I was the one yelling and crying. I said no. I was embarrassed. I imagine she knew I was lying, because my nose and face must have been red. But she pretended to believe me. I don't have anything negative to say about her. Her full name was Corina. She was neutral in our lives. No love, no hate, just someone I got to know a little better when I was an adult. And even then, I didn't really know her.

I don't know how my mother got money to buy fabric for our school uniforms. When my father left us, we had no means of support. Papa was a tailor and worked all the time to feed us. He was a very good tailor, and made clothes for men, women, and children. *Campesinos* paid him in bags of beans, rice, corn, and vegetables.

He was also the church pastor. Everyone wanted to help the young pastor and tailor feed his children. Everyone loved him. He was a religious man. But more than that, he was a good man.

Well, after he left us, all this ended. We lived off the charity of whoever wanted to help us. This wasn't easy because everyone around was also poor and struggling. The main help papa used to get was from congregants of other churches. At first, these people wanted to take some of us away from our mother, to help her. But she wouldn't do that. Not yet.

My mother was young and pretty. After a while she started to distance herself from the people of the churches. She'd smoke and go to dances. These "Capital sins" were not tolerated by the churches in these other communities. So they withdrew their support.

When my father was very young, before he met my mother, he had a son named Felix. When my father died, this young man came to live with us, to help somehow. He was about 16 years old. He tried to learn to sew, using our father's sewing machine. But that didn't work. Mama sold the sewing machine to buy food.

Felix decided to move to Nagua, to see if he could get a job and help us. At that time, it took 5 hours to get from our village to Nagua. Felix lived with friends of our father. But he couldn't help us. This family owned a store and Felix worked for them. In exchange, they sent him to school. He was an excellent student. He won a scholarship to attend university in Santiago. He became a lawyer. We didn't see him again for many, many years. He didn't forget us, he was just struggling for his own life. He didn't have any money to give us. Maybe that is why he stayed away. Also, there was no phone or mail service to remote villages like La Catalina. Only horses and mules and cows and us.

We lost something else when my father left us. Love. He was tender and patient and showered us with hugs and kisses. He was a unique human being. When I was a young woman and already a little bit in control of my life, I went back to visit the remote village where I was born. The house and land were gone. But there were some relatives still living there. And many, many "friends." The same friends and relatives that turned their back on us when our mother became a "sinner."

But I needed to face them again. Mainly, I needed to hear them talk about my father. Yes, I needed that very much. These people would hug me and with tears in their eyes would tell me that he was a Saint. That I have his eyes. I feel in my heart that they are telling the truth. Also, I feel that whatever little goodness is in me, I got it from him. (Sorry, mother). I do have things from my mother also, good and bad. But from him, only good. Papa was a noble and honest man. He was tender and patient with us. He always stopped our mother from beating us. This is what my dear Aunt Fresa tells me. He didn't believe in physical punishment; he couldn't hurt a bird.

Aside from the physical necessities, I imagine that when we lost him, we were left like little birds, without direction or source of protection. Years later, my mother told me that I was very attached to him. When he came home from church and sat down at his sewing machine, he would place me on his shoulders. My sister Esperanza was the eldest girl. She was 7 when Papa left us. Mama was a remarkable and strong woman. She really loved just one man, my father. Afterward, there were other men in her life, but these men served a purpose. She needed them. But she was always proud. Her inner strength was obvious to all of us. She demanded and commanded obedience. She didn't have to hit us constantly in order to get us to behave. Just a look was enough. Her eyes penetrated us.

In her later years, when we were all adults, she became very concerned about public opinion. "It's not what you do," she'd tell us. "It's what it looks like that matters."

When my sister and I visited Mama, to see our children, she never wanted us to have male friends visit.

"The neighbors would think they are your lovers," she'd tell us, "You have to watch your reputation." We feared crossing her. One time I tried. I told her, "Mama, but that is the way I see it." I walked away from her. She followed me, grabbed my shoulder, and turned me around. "What did you say?"

"Nothing, Mama." Wow. The force of those eyes!

Mama was a woman of duty, a woman of valor. When Felicia, Esperanza, and I needed to work and couldn't care for our children, Mama was there. The grandchildren loved her dearly. But they also feared her.

She'd send them out to play after their homework and chores.

"But whatever you do," she'd tell them, "Do not sweat."

Can you imagine, in a tropical country, with the air heavy and hot, trying to keep from sweating?

Whatever her eccentricities, I have sympathy for my mother. Her own mother died when she was a little child. Her aunt's sister, Nenena, raised her and kept her until she married my father. Then my father died and left her with all of us. After a couple of years trying to keep us all together, my mother gave up. She distributed us to relatives and friends — households that could feed us and send us to school. This was the norm for poor families. It was a matter of survival. But that was the beginning of our detachment as siblings. Mama just kept the younger boys, Rafael and Freddy.

Esperanza, Felicia, and I went to Nenena, the woman who raised Mama after her mother died. Sometimes I wonder about that decision.

(II)

Nenena

(II)

Nenena

The final morning in my mother's house I got up before the hens and the roosters. I needed to do a few things. By now, I was around 6 years old. I snuck out of the house and took a very slow walk down my beautiful path leading to the river. I talked to my wild beautiful flowers along the way. I told them to wait for me, that I didn't want to leave, but Mama thought we should go, for our own well-being. (Those were her words when we protested). I told my flowers that Mama couldn't keep us together because we ate too much and she didn't have money or a good man to help her. When I reached the river I sat down. This was my place. The river and I knew that. I explained my situation to the river. The river answered me, just like the flowers replied to me, with their strong fragrance. The river was extra melodious that morning. It was so, so gentle and calming to me to be there.

I don't know how long I sat by the river. The next thing I remember was my mother yelling at me.

"What do you think you're doing? You know you have to leave!"

"OK Mama," I said. "Goodbye river," I whispered. "I will see you soon."

On the way back up my lovely path, I reached the gardenia bush. I had forgotten all about it! "Goodbye dear white gardenias, I will see you soon." I wanted to say goodbye to the coconut palm, the grape vines, the almond tree, the orange and lemon trees, the gandules vines, the corn, tomatoes, and beans. And I also wanted to say goodbye to the gentle and generous cow. It had been so good to us. But my mother stood next to me. I had no choice but to join Esperanza and Felicia. That is all I remember from that morning. I don't remember feeling sadness at leaving behind my brothers, my home, or my mother.

To get to Nenena's house in those days, we needed to walk for a couple of hours to Cabrera. We crossed two rivers with rocks of all shapes and sizes. I hopped from rock to rock. After that, I don't remember anything of the journey, but I imagine that someone drove us from Cabrera to San Felipe. San Felipe is a village close to Pimentel, where Nenena's house stood.

I remember the first time I saw Nenena's house. It was early evening, but the sun was still shining. The house was huge and imposing. I remember the house, but I don't remember anyone receiving us. I would soon understand that the house was situated on a very large piece of land, a working farm. Nenena had about 10 men working the fields; they would come every evening for their pay.

Although I cannot remember my mother as a young woman, I do remember Nenena. She was tall and elegant, and she always moved like a queen. She walked like she was a movie star. A frustrated movie star.

Nenena was a hard, cruel woman. She never had children. She had a few husbands, some died, some divorced her. In her youth, she was beautiful and arrogant. When she took us in, she was probably in her mid-forties.

At mealtime, she'd tell us we had to learn to be "ladies." Esperanza, Felicia, and I would sit at the long table with her and her husband at the time, Don Turin.

Don Turin dressed formally in a beige suit and kept his head down. I think he seriously feared Nenena. He hardly spoke when we were around. He certainly didn't stand up to protect us.

We arrived at Nenena's without the slightest idea of what it meant to have manners or to "be a lady." Mama didn't have time or the inclination to teach us that. She was too busy trying to get our daily meal. Well, Nenena had both the time and the inclination. And so she did. We had to learn to eat with fork and knife and to say, "Could you please pass the sauce," and "May I be excused?"

Esperanza, the oldest, did better than Felicia and I, as far as dealing with Nenena. She was very careful to follow Nenena's instructions. I wasn't. I would start eating with the fork, which was very difficult for me. Then, without realizing it, I would grab a piece of meat with my fingers. Puah! Nenena would slap my hand with her ruler. The pain brought tears to my eyes, but I wasn't allowed to cry, so I would bite my lip. Each time she hit me it sent food flying. I had to clean up the food, return to the table, and resume eating with a fork and knife. If I stopped eating, Nenena would hit me again.

As bad as it was for me, it was worse for Felicia. She arrived at the table already crying. She knew what was coming. Oh, the irony. We had food, but we didn't want to eat. We were afraid. My poor sister Felicia suffered so much. After a month or so of this torture, we got to the point where the hand hitting wasn't too often. Only sometimes, when we would forget and instead of using the nicely folded napkin, we would clean our mouths with our arms or our skirts. Then she'd hit us with the ruler and we'd force back the tears.

After dinner, we'd massage our arms and hands with cool water and cry.

Sometimes we would go into the kitchen and the maid, Dona Maria, would give us food. She knew how it was for us. She feared talking to us and we were afraid to talk to her. Only when Nenena napped or travelled could we relax and be happy for a little while.

Esperanza did better with the table manners, but then Nenena turned on her.

Esperanza was 10 years old when we arrived there. She was so beautiful and fresh and with a natural mischievous look on her face. She had a happy nature. She loved to sing and dance, even without music. She was very vain also. She knew she was pretty, and she was happy about it.

It seemed like Nenena resented Esperanza's beauty and youth. She tormented her in front of Don Turin. She beat Esperanza with a big wooden stick she kept for that purpose. When Esperanza cried, she would hit her more, because Nenena said she was crying so that Don Turin would protect her. But if my sister didn't cry, she would hit her because it meant that she was showing off so that Don Turin would see how brave she was. Nenena's beatings left my beautiful sister with bruises on her face, arms and back. Nenena beat her at least twice a week.

Meanwhile, Nenena beat Felicia every day. Felicia was so fragile and scared all the time. She wet the bed at night. We slept together, and every night our bed was wet and smelly. Early in the morning we would take the mattress out, behind some bushes to dry. But Nenena saw everything.

Felicia would get up sobbing. She couldn't stop. She knew what was coming. My poor baby. Even today I resent this crazy, cruel woman. Nenena beat us with whatever she could grab. When she beat us with dry branches from the palm trees, our skin would itch and burn for hours. If we wet our bodies to try and wash it off, the itching would get worse. The branches were like an octopus, with lots of pointed tentacles. Such was our life at the mansion.

This big, ugly house had many rooms. Felicia and I slept in one bedroom. Esperanza shared a room with the maid. There was one room that Nenena kept closed with a giant lock on the door. No one was allowed there. Only crazy Nenena would go there with her patients. Yes, she had patients. Her patients were mainly crazy people.

Yes, she was a witch. A real witch. *A real, real witch.*

I saw people being brought up to her house. The person would be tied down and screaming, foaming at the mouth. Well, Nenena would take that person into this mysterious room, stay there for many hours, and come out of there walking and talking with this person. I saw this with my own eyes many times.

After the patient went home, Nenena would go into the large kitchen and order Dona Maria to make a concoction for her. She used a very large container and placed many different herbs and roots and let it boil for hours. This was the "medicine" for the crazy people. Nenena also prepared mysterious looking bags and powders for farmers and people who could pay her to put a curse on someone or on someone's business. This was scary stuff. We were so afraid of this woman.

One day I decided to write a letter to our mother, begging her to come and take us back. It wasn't easy to send a letter or a message. If you had a letter, you'd have to wait until someone from the house was going to Pimentel, and send the letter with that person, who would bring it to the post office. And the only person that traveled to Pimentel was Nenena. There was no mailman and no telephones.

So of course Nenena read my letter. She knew everything. That time, the beating I got was so bad that

I couldn't walk. She hit me so hard and so long that my legs were swollen and painful for weeks. We were trapped. After that, we didn't try to write to Mama. And, Mama never came to visit. Maybe she didn't have the money for the car fare from Cabrera.

Nenena traveled to other towns to buy funky stuff that she used to make her concoctions. Or to follow her husband. Don Turin was a dentist, and kept his office in Pimentel. (As a side note, I recently learned that quiet, unassuming Don Turin was something of a Don Juan. He had other lovers in Cabrera. I'm not sure if Nenena knew this when we lived under her roof.)

We were happiest when Nenena was away.

She was a witch, and she was also a businesswoman. She was always buying and selling things. She converted a large room in her mansion into a bodega. She hired a young woman to run the store. This woman never spoke to us, nor us to her. We called her the mystery woman. But whenever Nenena traveled, she'd close the store and the mystery woman would vanish. For some reason she let go of the mystery woman. Then she brought over our brother Mario to tend the store. We were so happy to see him because we figured now we may have a chance to run away with him. Nenena didn't give us much of an opportunity to talk to our brother. She kept him by her side, or in the store, where we were not allowed to enter. Nevertheless, Mario became aware of our misery and the physical abuse. He decided to punish her. So, the only means available to him was the store. He started to give away all the merchandise, very slowly, every day. Whenever a very poor family came over to purchase something (and there were many, many poor families), he would just give them whatever they needed. Well, to make a long story short, the store went down. Nenena got very, very angry, but she wouldn't dare hit him. She just took him to Pimentel and from there sent him to our mother. One way ticket. Ahhh, we were devastated. But we hoped that any day now our mother would show up to take us home. We were sure Mario was going to tell her about us. But, no, Mama never came over.

I may not have been able to use a fork, but I could climb anything. I was like a spider. When I discovered the bodega, I made plans. I'd wait for Nenena to go away. Then I'd sneak into the bodega, climb to the top shelf, and steal a can of condensed milk. I'd hide in the latrine and drink the whole can. Then I'd throw the empty can in the latrine and push it under with a stick.

It was gross, but good also. I still love condensed milk, and it brings a smile to my face even today. This one, Nenena never discovered. I was able to beat the beast. *Hallelujah!*

I don't think Mama knew our suffering. I don't think so. Years went by, and we didn't hear from Mama, or she from us.

I forgot to mention that this new place had so many fruit trees all around us. So many. The mangos, oranges, lemons, and grapes would rot on the trees and on the ground. No one would dare to take any. Well, my wild nature insisted that since I had beaten the beast once, I could do it again. So one rainy afternoon, while Nenena took her siesta, I scampered up a mango tree to pick two fruits that were just too tempting, just so ripe and inviting. I grabbed the first mango, but the branches were slippery because of the rain.

I fell. I fell face down on the mango tree roots. I had cuts on my lips and my tongue. I was bleeding so much, but the fear didn't let me feel any pain. I was just trying to find a place to hide until the blood stopped. Well, it's a good thing that someone found me. One of the day laborers stopped by to pick up some seeds. He didn't see me, but he saw a trail of blood from the tree to a big bush that was behind one of the pigs' sties. There I was, letting the rain wash away the blood, so much blood. He took me by the arm and I let him do whatever. I was too scared to think. He took me to the kitchen and Dona Maria went to get Nenena.

Ah, Nenena. But you will be surprised. I think she was so overcome by all the blood pooling around me. She probably thought I was going to die. She just took me by the arm. Took me to the room. Yes, *that* room. The first thing she did was light a candle. I thought she was going to burn me with it. I was terrified.

She took the candle, made some signs with it, then put it down and started to make signs over me. She took a towel and wrapped me up, like a candy. I was shaking. She then took some concoction and told me to drink it. All this time, she didn't seem threatening to me. She was just intent on stopping the blood. I really think she thought that I was a goner. So, she gave me something to drink. It was very bitter. Now that I know better, I think there was alcohol in it. I tried to drink but I was really drinking my own blood. She then took an extremely bitter powder, asked me to open my mouth and placed it there and covered it with a very cool piece of something. She told me to close my mouth, to sit down and not open my mouth or move my tongue. Then she turned away from me. After an eternity, she turned to face me again. Meanwhile, she had been on her knees praying, I think. Or calling some help from hell. It could have been either one.

By this time, I had stopped shaking. The bleeding had stopped. I was falling asleep on my chair. It was a very comfortable rocking chair. Her own. It was the Queen's rocking chair.

After a very long time, she took me by the hand and walked me to the bathroom. She took off all my clothes. She wrapped me up again in a large towel and told me to go to my room and put on my pajamas and do my prayers, without moving my tongue or opening my mouth. She told me to go to sleep. "Tomorrow," she said, "we will talk."

Well, I had nightmares that night. I was grateful to her for saving my life. At the same time, I was frightened. I couldn't believe that I had seen the room.

I couldn't wait until my mouth healed and I could talk and tell my sisters.

Early the next morning Nenena spoke to me. "Don't brush your teeth," she said. "Just get dressed and go to the breakfast table. "How can I eat?" I thought to myself. My mouth had swelled up like a balloon. But I obeyed. As soon as she saw me getting dressed, Nenena left the room. As I sat, Nenena gave me a large glass of orange juice and a cut mango. The irony! I knew the pain would be unbearable if I ate and drank; but if I refused I knew she'd beat me. So I sipped the juice. My tongue and lips burned. I couldn't continue. I just looked at everyone with tears streaming down my cheeks. Still, trying to be obedient, I took my nicely folded napkin up toward my face. But then I stopped. *"Oh no,"* I thought, *"What if I stain the napkin with my blood?"* I glanced up at Nenena, to see if she was coming toward me. But she was sitting calmly, eating her soft boiled egg and talking to her husband. So I risked the napkin and cleaned my face. There was no blood, just tears and the water from my nose. I sat very still, looking down and waiting for her next command. Or beating.

She didn't beat me then. After she finished her breakfast, she mixed a white powder in a glass of water and ordered me to drink it. I did. It felt good going down my throat. I wanted more, but I knew well enough not to ask. Nenena handed me a bag of ice and a towel. "Go to bed and put this against your mouth. Don't talk or move your tongue."

I slept the whole day. I think I had a fever, because I woke up freezing and trembling. The sheets and my pajamas were wet. Dona Maria visited in the afternoon with a bowl of consommé. I was starving, but I couldn't eat. Too painful. Dona Maria brought a glass of green water and told me to drink it. I went to sleep again.

The following morning, I wanted to eat. I was feeling better. My mouth was still swollen, but it didn't hurt as much. For a whole week, I was fed homemade yogurt and homemade ice cream. They were so delicious and they didn't bother my tongue or my lips. It was a blessing. I felt like I could love this monster for giving me these treats.

To this day, I still have three scars on my tongue. I never tried to climb one of her trees again. Life kept on going at the scary mansion. We were growing up and enduring our undefined prison sentence. By now we could walk like "ladies" without breaking into a run, to eat with a fork and knife, to keep our eyes fixed on the floor and to remain silent in Nenena's presence.

Nenena beat Esperanza and Felicia more than she beat me. I don't know why. She only seriously beat me three times. (This, of course, is aside from the daily ruler hittings). There was the day I wrote the letter to my mother, the day I told her my hips hurt, and the day I had a fight with a boy at school.

According to Nenena, only adult women have hips. Little girls cannot pretend to have hips. So when I said that my hips hurt, Nenena said she needed to teach me a lesson. And she beat me.

The day I had a fight with a boy at school, the teacher gave me a note to give to Nenena. I don't know why I gave it to her, but I did. After Nenena read the note she said, "Young lady, tomorrow morning I will go to school with you." I stayed awake all night and kept Felicia awake too. "What do you think she'll do?" I whispered to Felicia over and over. Poor Felicia just kept on crying.

The next morning we had to go to the table, sit and eat like proper ladies, thank Nenena and get ready to go to school. My sisters and I walked in front; Nenena brought up the rear like a Sargent. I remember that I was mortified trying to figure out how to walk. If I went too fast, that would upset Nenena. If I went too slowly, that would upset her too. It was a cool, nice morning. The country road to the school was very pleasant. On both sides, there were big open fields, with all kinds of animals grazing. The fields were lush and green and birds sang and called around us. Normally, the three of us would run down this road, just feeling free and enjoying the early morning life. But today, all this beauty was an insult. This precious morning, we were suffering.

When we arrived at school, Nenena went straight to the teacher and had a few words with him. He stared at me. I was shaking. Nenena unfurled a long stick from her purse. It was freshly cut with little green leaves still attached to it. As she shook it open I thought, *I am safe in here. She won't beat me in front of the entire class.*

I was wrong.

She grabbed me by my skinny arm and started to whip me, right there in front of everyone. The teacher stood by, the students sat at their desks and Nenena whipped me over and over again. I cried from the pain and the humiliation. When she finished she held me by the wrist and told me, "You and your sisters will never go out for recess again. Never. You will stay inside and study. Now go to your seat."

I had to sit down, take out my books and pretend the beating hadn't happened. None of the other students would look at me. It was a very quiet and somber morning inside that classroom. My sisters and I continued to cry and we didn't have a tissue or anything to clean our eyes. We were afraid to use our skirts to wipe our faces, because the monster could come out from behind the door and beat us. So the tears kept sliding down our cheeks and onto our notebooks.

The next time my "dear" professor sent a note home, I feared another beating. The note said that I didn't know my times tables. Nenena knew we were afraid of her "medicine room" so she locked me in there, to cure me of being stupid. It was a dark, windowless room. Nenena lit two creepy candles before she left me in there. The candlelight cast shadows over a brutal collection of figures: some with rope around their necks, some with pins inserted into their eyes or mouths, some placed head first into a container. I think the figures were made of wax. She also had pictures and sculptures of saints with big eyes and half smiles.

I wasn't thinking about my multiplication tables. I knew I wanted to study this room completely, regardless of my fear. I wanted to tell my sisters every last detail. So I memorized the look and posture of each figure. After a long time, I heard Nenena's footsteps approaching the room. Without opening the door she said, "Do you know your tables?"

"Not yet," I said.

"Then you cannot leave." I heard her footsteps receding as she walked away. At that point I decided to learn the multiplication tables. And I did. Nenena let me out of her witch's den. But then she started locking me in all sorts of other rooms. I remember one room with holes between the wooden planks. I used to see all kinds of eyes staring back at me through those holes. Green, blue, red, yellow, orange...that was scary. I think that was just my imagination. There can't be so many eye colors.

Esperanza suffered the most lasting damage from the Nenena years. She was forced to stay longer than me and Felicia. After about 2 years, we were sent back to Mama. I guess it took Mama 2 years to get the money together to come and take us home. We were lucky to be going home, but poor Piran (our nickname for Esperanza) wasn't so lucky. I can only guess that Nenena convinced Mama to let her keep Esperanza longer. To completely break her. Despite the beatings, Esperanza was a little wild. She kept getting more and more beautiful and developed.

Nenena had informally adopted a son years earlier. This young man was ugly and bad. She paid for him to attend some military boarding school. He returned to Nenena's house when he was 18 years old. When Esperanza was 14 years old, Nenena decided to give Esperanza to him as a wife. When Mama heard this news she went to Nenena's house. The two women had some words and Mama took Esperanza away from that awful place.

But it was complicated for Esperanza. She was a married woman. Mentally she was only about 10 or 11 but she looked like she was 18. Esperanza had a lot of boyfriends during this time and Mama struggled with her. After her prison time at Nenena's house, who could blame her wild behavior? And God only knew what she suffered while she was married to the stupid son.

When we returned to Mama's house, it was a reunion of sorts; Mama had also brought back Mario and Manases. I'm sure I was happy to see them, but my true love at that time was for my gardenia bush, my path to the river, the bird songs and the rush of river water. It had only been 2½ years, but so much had changed. My gardenia bush was gone, the path was neglected and weeds had overtaken the flowers I had left behind. A few trees remained: coconut, almond, and *higuero,* but they produced so little fruit. Nevertheless I found a new spot on the river bank and put my feet in. Suddenly, I was brought back to that magical place. I forgot everything bad, all of the Nenenas and the bad teachers and the switches and the rulers. I was at my river again, my feet in the fresh, cool waters.

But things hadn't improved for Mama. My grandfather had left. My mother had a new boyfriend, but he was poor like the rest of us. Mama couldn't feed all of us. So once again, she looked for houses to place us in. My sisters and I begged her not to send us back to Nenena. We swore we'd drown ourselves in the river before going back to that crazy woman's house. Mama found a different place for me, where I could work as a servant, cleaning and caring for the children in exchange for food, shelter, and schooling. I was 8 years old.

(III)

Alba

(III)

Alba

After Nenena's torture chamber, I was happy to work as a servant girl. Mama sent me to work in my Godmother Alba's house in Cabrera, caring for her two children (she was pregnant with a third), cleaning, and running errands. Mama chose an old uncle of hers, Papa Cedo, to take me to Cabrera. (I never liked him). His wife, Mama Mecha, was a different story. She was so sweet and good and tender. I loved her as an aunt.

Aside from Papa Cedo taking me, I have no memory of arriving at Alba's. For everything that I can remember, there are so many empty spaces where I cannot remember anything.

Alba didn't abuse me. Living in her house I don't remember being sad or lonely or wishing to be someplace else. But we were taught never to question.

Children's feelings weren't important at that time, I guess. I accepted that. Alba treated me as her servant but she was not cruel. She worked hard and wanted others around her to work hard as well. I knew my responsibilities and tried to be on my best behavior. I wanted to be a good employee.

The children were 2 and 1 when I arrived. They were precious. I fell in love with them, and I still love them. I used to love to sit and rock them to sleep. I was so skinny and they were big, healthy boys. It wasn't easy for me to fit them on my lap or carry them on my hips, but I did.

Each morning, I'd rise early and make tea for the kids from dried leaves behind the house. Then I had to change and wash their cloth diapers. After that I'd prepare and feed them breakfast and then I'd rush off to school.

Alba decided to set up a small factory at home. We made caramels that Alba sold at the *purperias* in town. I had to get up at 4 AM. At that time, Homero was living with us. He was a boy about my age who was the son of Alba's husband from a previous woman. The two of us had to help make these *caramelos* and Homero was responsible for distribution.

There was more work now, but I don't remember ever feeling tired or overwhelmed. I just did everything automatically. In those years, I arrived at school late with my fingernails (and tummy) full of caramel. Of course I didn't have time to do my hair like the other girls. All my teachers knew about my life, so they never gave me a hard time.

I'd fly down Calle Duarte every morning, racing to school. My hair streamed behind me like a wild girl. People in town all knew me, and so they'd say, "Buenos Dias, Doris. It's late already."

Alba's husband was a nice man. I liked him. I used to dream of being able to call him Papa, just like his kids did. He was a military man and sometimes he got stationed in other towns. Sometimes he'd bring us along. We'd go to school in these new towns and we'd meet new people. When I was with girls my age and I had the kids with me I'd say, "Okay kids, let's go. Papa is waiting for us." I wanted them to think that he was my father too. They didn't know us, or our past, so I could pretend.

I don't think he ever spoke to me. Unless it was to tell me to bring him something from the kitchen or any other place. But I felt that he was good, it was a feeling.

The years passed smoothly. I did my work, went to school, and made a bunch of friends, among them my dearest best friend, Dominicana. In another chapter, I will speak of my dear friends. I had so many. They felt like sisters and brothers to me.

I can't remember if I missed my mother or my siblings. Even though Mario, my older brother, used to walk from Catalina to Cabrera every day to go to school, he rarely stopped by to see me.

Alba's life wasn't easy either. She struggled to make ends meet as the wife of a policeman. And she had three kids plus me and Homero to feed. I guess that's why she was always trying to do business. She had the caramel factory. Another time she sold men's shirts and socks from the house. Then she had a bodega. When she had the bodega she'd return home with a brown bag full of coins. She'd lock the coins in her bedroom dresser. I'd pick the lock and take coins to buy ice cream after school. I had the feeling that Homero was also helping himself. Alba never knew this, of course, and I should be ashamed about this, but I am not. I needed to buy ice cream and no one ever gave me a coin.

My life as a babysitter was kind of okay. I carried out my errands, took care of my kids, and played in the big backyard, where we had so many banana trees and herbs. I used to love to sneak behind one of these trees to read my romantic illustrated novelas. I don't know where I got them. My other love was going to school. At school, I was a normal kid.

From 3rd level to 8th level, our small group of close friends studied and played together. My friends knew I didn't have the freedom and means that they did, but they always tried to include me in their adventures. Alba only allowed me to go to Maritza or Dominicana's houses. I must admit, I was a bit wild, instead of walking out though the door, I would jump out over the veranda.

I really don't have any negative feelings toward Alba for the way she treated me. I was simply her maid and she was responsible for me. She did try to save my soul. She made me go to church and she baptized me. That was generous of her.

By the time we moved to 6th level, our small group at school was gaining a reputation as "troublemakers" or "wild." We were 12 girls: Migdalia Acosta, Zoila del Rosario, Adalgiza, Ana Julia, Charo Ramon, Maritza Santos, Maritza Martinez (we had two Maritzas), Dinora Eusebio (Loa), Altagracia, Griselide and myself. (There was one more girl, but I can't remember her name.)

We always played together, making up lies, copying each other's homework, feeding answers to each other during class. During recess, some of us would lock ourselves in Maritza Santos' grandma's house, take off our clothes and dance, just like we imagined in the movies.

This dancing business stopped because Arnaldo, Zoila's brother, caught us. He spied on us through a hole in the wall and told our teacher. Our teacher punished us, but the punishments were a breeze (Write something over and over, staying inside during recess, etc.). I was used to so much worse. After this, the school director,

Sr. Marte, named us *Los Fosforitos* (little matchsticks). He didn't mean it kindly. Sr. Marte was always very serious and sometimes looked angry.

When we advanced to 8th level, we met our dear new teacher. His name was Cuchito. He was a very young and serious man. He knew our bad reputation, so on the first day of class he talked to us.

"Senoritas, you are already young ladies, so I expect you to behave as such." Well, we tried, and he was so nice (and handsome), but we couldn't do it. He was tender, patient, stern *and* approachable. He tried everything. "You have so much potential," he'd tell us. "Think about your dreams. Dream big." He believed in the power of education. "Continue your studies..." he'd tell us, "...even if that means leaving your family and moving somewhere else. I know you are smart and good young women." We all loved and respected him. We couldn't help it: he was like a good big brother.

During 8th level, Dominicana and I decided to play a prank on Loa. Loa was the most serious and proper of the girls. Dominicana and I filled our heads with fantasies from our romance novels. I stashed my worn romance novels in the outdoor latrine at Alba's house. I'd read and re-read those lovely stories about Prince Charming and beautiful girls with long, flowing hair and the impossible love that always ended in a passionate kiss.

Well, Dominicana and I wrote an anonymous love letter to Loa. We wrote things like:

I want to kiss your lips passionately

I want to transport you to an island where only you and I can live.

I want to taste the nectar of your lips.

I want to carry you in my arms and protect you forever.

We signed the letter W.H. and put it under her books. (Today we talk about it, we don't know why we did this cruel thing to poor Loa, nor why we signed it "W.H.")

When Loa found the letter, she started to sob and to shake. Our sweet Cuchito lifted the letter from her hands. She was holding it like a piece of burning wood.

"Who wrote this?" he asked.

No one answered.

But soon enough Dominicana and I started to cry. We felt terrible for poor Loa.

"No one is leaving my classroom until someone confesses."

Of course we told the truth. Our punishment was to write 1,000 times: *We are very sorry. We won't ever do this again. It was very cruel to do this to you. Loa, please forgive us.*

And she did. She was and is an angel.

We graduated from 8th level. It was a very strange feeling. My friends hung out at the park, sat on the benches, went to the river, picnicked at the beach, or just chatted in front of their houses. Not me. Alba gave me more work to do.

Meanwhile, I was developing physically, but I don't think that my emotional development was in tune with my body. I became rebellious. I was restless. I was 16 years old. It was 1961.

This was the same year that the dictator Trujillo was assassinated by his own men (with backing by the US government). It was a very scary time throughout the country. I remember that almost every adult man in Cabrera was sent to guard the beaches and the main ports. They carried machetes and knives to their posts.

After a couple of months and after hundreds of people had been killed (and many more were in jail), the country started to calm down. The feeling was like when there has been a terrible earthquake and people start to put their belongings in place, to mourn their loved ones and to be grateful to be alive and free.

The country had been under such a strict and severe dictatorship that for some it took years to learn to live without being afraid. All of this I learned later on. At 16 years of age, I didn't understand our political situation. Also, Cabrera had no television, few radios and not a lot of newspapers.

I learned about the dictatorship and its aftermath in bits and pieces. Years later, when I was already living in New York, I learned that Alba's husband had been assassinated. He was stationed in another town. He had started complaining about prison conditions, about the government, and about corruption. Someone got fed up. One clear summer day, a man came up from behind him, took his gun, and shot him in the head. He died on the sidewalk. His killer then walked into a beauty salon beside Alba's husband's dead body.

"You saw nothing," he said. "If you talk, you'll be next."

This is what Alba learned and this is what she told me. But officially, no one saw anything and no one said anything.

Both during the dictatorship and after, this kind of thing was normal. People got killed or disappeared. People were scared into silence.

One morning when I was cleaning, Alba told me, "I'm sending you back."

"Sending me back?" I didn't have a return address. Plus, I had been with her family for 8 years, which felt like a lifetime.

"I'm working on that. But you're too wild now. I don't know what to do with you."

I didn't take her seriously. An uncle had come by years earlier and told Alba that Mama had moved to the Capital. We didn't know where, but Alba researched it and found Esperanza in the nearby town of Nagua. Esperanza was living with a man who owned a small restaurant. He was using her as his unpaid employee and as his lover. So she decided to send me to Esperanza.

I don't remember saying goodbye to anyone, not even my dear friends. I didn't understand how this could be happening. I was already 16, I should remember. But I don't. I do remember the morning I left. At 5:30, I stood by myself on Alba's small veranda waiting for the daily bus to Nagua. I remember standing there with a small box that contained all my possessions. I wanted

Alba or someone (anyone!) to get up and say goodbye to me. Or to tell me, "No, it is all a mistake! Please stay!" Or at the very least, "If they don't treat you well, you can always come back." But nobody came and I got on the bus by myself. Maybe Alba was sorry to see me go, though for some reason, she needed to send me home.

As an adult, I reconnected with Alba and her children, 3 boys and 2 girls. I still love them and am happy when I see them. They also love me. Alba and I are friends now. I admire her for her strength and for teaching me to work hard and for trying to save my soul. When I see her, I really have feelings for her. Right now, she is not doing too well. Her mind is not all-together. Supposedly it is Alzheimer's. But she recognizes everyone and makes sense sometimes. I go and visit her at her daughter's house. I hold her hands and look into her eyes. I really care about her.

(IV)

Cabrera

(IV)

Cabrera

Even though I was born in a distant and poor little village about 2 or 3 miles from Cabrera, my love has always been for Cabrera.

In the 1950s and 1960s, Cabrera was a small town of about 150 people. Everyone knew each other. It had two named streets: Calle Duarte (where I lived with Alba) and Calle Independencia. Calle Duarte ran from the entrance to the town all the way down to El Cabo, named for the surrounding rock formation. Craggy cliffs framed a deep and angry Atlantic Ocean. When, for whatever reason, people needed to end their lives, they'd go there and jump.

In town, there were 4 or 5 small and narrow streets, but without names. We had a post office with just one employee and one telephone to send and receive cablegrams. We had a police station with a few policemen. One of these policemen was a married man, with 5 or 6 children, who was in love with me. He used to tell people that "When that little girl grows up, I am going to marry her."

We also had a Catholic church and a priest. Every week Alba would send me to church to pray and to confess. I loved it, because I never even got close to the church. I didn't like the priest, I didn't think I had anything to confess, and more importantly, I didn't believe in such things. The opportunity to be free, to have an hour just for myself, was great. I would go to the park, where there were many, many almond trees. These trees were so cute, not too tall, with many beautiful branches. I would climb up my favorite one. I liked this tree because it had the most branches and leaves. I'd hide there, to recline in one of those loving branches, eat almonds, and watch the world go by. After a while, I'd climb down and walk home to Alba. I was very serious and relaxed, just to show how clean and saintly I was feeling.

Sorry, my Catholic friends. It is just me.

Cabrera was a poor town. Just like Garcia Marquez's Macondo, in *One Hundred Years of Solitude*. Everyone did what they could to get by. Most people lived off the land and the sea: working as farmers, cattle ranchers, and fishermen. Some people headed off on horseback to neighboring villages to work as teachers. Some women – like Alba – made candies, ice cream, and clothing to help make ends meet.

We were like a big family. People left their doors open and kids played in the streets and at the rivers by themselves, even at night. Some people didn't know how to write or read. Our only school got to the 8th level, no further. We had three large stores (large compared to other smaller *purperias* or *tiendas*), where you could purchase everything from Aspirin to shoe shine. Monsito Martinez owned one of the stores. He was Maritza Martinez's father. Alberto Jose Namis owned another one. He had a few kids and one of the boys was in our class. This boy was handsome. Eladio Acosta owned the third store. He was Migdalia's father. He owned a store and a bar. These three families and Dominicana's family were the town's wealthiest. They owned land and cattle and stores. They were all good and simple people. As a young girl I didn't have any interaction with these adults, just their children. But I don't ever remember feeling that these families were treated differently from any others.

The reason I compare my loving Cabrera to Macondo is because of how it has changed. Foreigners and tourism came to my beloved Cabrera. With this money flowing in, Cabrera saw some benefits: a hospital, more job options, a new primary school, even a high school. Each house has a telephone and electricity, and most people have cell phones. Now, instead of horseback and buses, people zip around on mopeds and big SUVs with tinted windows. Of course, all of these vehicles couldn't fit down the narrow streets of my Cabrera, so they have been transformed into large and modern streets, complete with street names and electric lighting at night.

Foreigners own most of the stores now and the coastline is crowded with gated mansions, hotels, and businesses. With this progress (regress?) came money, drugs, and violence. Most people have guns to protect themselves or guards to keep watch over them. Even so, I have one friend who was savagely beaten and robbed in her own home. She survived this attack but was left traumatized. Another friend had her home invaded and robbed several times. My cousin, during his afternoon siesta at home, was robbed and beaten. A foreign woman disappeared. Months later the police found her safe deposit box in another town. Her body was never recovered.

I believe that this new reality has proven particularly dubious for the young people. For some, the flow of money has brought opportunity and freedom. They live good professional lives. But for others, the rich men and women in the mansions pay them for their pleasures and to do their dirty work. They give the young people drugs and money. It is dangerous and sad.

Nevertheless, many of my friends remain devoted to Cabrera. Even though they became professionals, and moved to the Capital, other larger towns, or, like me, to other countries, they never forgot. They support poorer families and friends still in Cabrera. They were also instrumental in founding the new hospital and schools. Our friends Arnaldo, Sergio, Rey and Tato belong to an organization that supports poor students to get a university education. Marina Garcia and Aulio Chevalier have also been tireless in their work to help Cabrera. They started a tradition called "Cabrerenos

Ausentes" where each July Cabrera natives are invited to return and celebrate our beloved town.

I went to Aristides Fiallo Cabral primary school. I loved it. At school, I could allow my imagination to fly and be free. There, my world was beautiful. I was a good student, always prepared for my lessons (though I don't remember studying!) I made my first real friendships there. With the exception of a few families, we were all poor (some more than others). But there was never, ever a distinction between us. We were just a bunch of friends.

Dominicana's friendship meant the world to me. She was the daughter of one of the richest families in town. Her father was very patriotic, even naming his daughter after his country. Domi is sweet and beautiful, inside and out. As soon as I met her mother, Dona Juana, I fell in love with her too. Dona Juana treated me with so much love and compassion.

Domi and I were both very romantic. We adored reading *novelas,* romance novels full of girls dreaming about hugging and kissing their Prince Charming. At school, we did everything together. After school, I would go home, do my domestic tasks, and ask Alba's permission to go to Domi's house so we could study together. Alba kept me on a tight leash. But she always let me go to Dominicana's house. We almost never studied. Instead we'd gossip and listen to love songs. Ha, ha. We fooled Alba.

Then there was my friend Maritza. Her family was well off, but not as wealthy as Domi's. Maritza and I bathed in the river together. Sometimes, the riverbank was the meeting place for all of our friends: Migdalia, Maritza Santos, Charo, Zoila, Maritza Martinez, Loa, Arnaldo, Tato, Ismael, Miguelito, Rey, Sergio and (the late) Majaso. There are others that I haven't seen in over 55 years, but I can't remember all their names.

Tato was the only male friend that Alba allowed me to see. He was a few years younger than me. But he was very mature and very sweet and caring. Most evenings, when I was rocking my 'children' to sleep, sitting in a rocking chair, he would come over, sit on the floor and keep me company. We would talk about life, school, friends, and I don't remember what, but it was always so pleasant and good to share with him. He was like a younger trusting brother to me. I loved him, and still love him very dearly. There were other boys at school, and casual friends, but I was shy and I never really spoke to them, unless it was at the school building.

When we finished the 8th grade, our education stopped. Cabrera didn't get its first high school until after I left. Some of my friends went to that high school, and then a few families moved to larger towns, so their children could continue their education. They became professionals: doctors, lawyers, even a priest.

After I put the kids to bed, I'd ask Alba's permission to go to Maritza's to study. She'd usually agree. But instead of studying, Maritza and I would sneak through the back door of her house and run to her farm. We'd untie two gentle horses and ride them into the night. Her parents owned big, big farms with open fields all around the house. Her family owned 5 square miles of gorgeous farmland that bordered the sea. We'd ride without saddles, holding onto the horses' manes, laughing and tearing through the fields, the sound of hooves and crashing waves all around us. It was divine to feel the warmth of the horses' bodies against our bodies. Just skin to skin. Each time we did that, I had a good night's sleep. That was our secret. We couldn't use a saddle because her mother or siblings would know, and they would stop us. I will talk about that in another chapter.

During the 8 years that I stayed with Alba, my mother never came to see me. I didn't think about this when I was young, but when I became a mother I reflected on this with sadness. Her home in La Catalina was a two hour walk from Cabrera.

Alba decided to baptize me. She knew my family was protestant, so she took it upon herself to save my soul. She brought me to her church and baptized me as a Catholic. Fine, no problem for me there. Religion is another issue which I may or may not talk about later. It's not an issue for me. But on that day, Alba became my godmother.

Well, getting back to my Mama, she never came or sent someone to see if I was still living or whatever. I still look for reasons. Maybe she didn't want to see me as a child maid? Could be. I was the only one of her children who didn't work for a relative. The others were slaving for the 'family.' Or they were slaving for some members of the church that wanted to help us. Or maybe she was too busy taking care of the two other boys, sons of the guy that gave her the cow.

One day, decades later, Mama and I were talking. We seemed to be in a good place, so I ventured, "When I was living with Alba, you never came over. Was there a reason?"

"That woman" she said, referring to Alba, "was too proud. I didn't like her."

My mother was very simple and shy. She was honest and hard working. After I became a woman and a mother, I learned to see my mother in a different light. I decided to understand her.

She had a very sad life. The only happiness she knew was those 10 years she was married to my father. I learned to see in her the strength that sustained her through all the tribulations life presented to her. She bore 10 children and fed all of us, until she couldn't any more. At 32 years old, my poor mother had already lost each and every one of her teeth.

Each night I'd sit in the rocking chair and sing each child to sleep. But there was something that happened during this time which was too painful for me to bring up with my mother.

When I was growing up, there weren't many cars on the streets of Cabrera. Alba lived on one of the two main streets, Calle Duarte. Every car that drove through Cabrera had to pass by this street and therefore, our house. One evening as I rocked Jose Ramon to sleep, thinking about what mischief I would do after the kids fell asleep, I saw an old pick-up truck driving in front of the house. Old, familiar furniture was piled up in the back, including a table and chairs painted blue and my black bed frame. It was my mother's furniture! I put Jose Ramon down and ran out to the street. I stared at that truck until it disappeared. I couldn't believe it. I couldn't believe my mother and my three younger siblings would have passed right by the house where I was working as a servant without stopping to say hello or goodbye. Where were they moving? I started sobbing. For the first time, I felt like an orphan, abandoned. I had never felt like this before.

My yelling and sobbing startled Alba and she followed me outside. I told her what I had seen. "You don't know what you're talking about," she told me. "You're seeing visions."

"I'm not! I swear!"

To placate me, Alba promised she'd investigate for me.

"Thank you, thank you!" I told her.

"Stop thanking me and just stop crying like a crazy woman! Pick up the child and don't scare him with your nonsense!"

True to her word, Alba found out what happened. I was right. It was my mother's items on that truck.

Mama sold the cow and the tiny piece of land our Papa left us. She had met this young man, Tonito, who promised to help her, but only if she followed him to another village called Los Ranchos, near Nagua. He promised that she could work the land and build a better life. Tonito had work lined up there for himself as well. He promised to help Mama with her younger boys and Felicia, who was living with her now. I don't know if my brothers Mario or Mananses knew about this moving adventure. I never, ever mentioned this to Mama. I couldn't do it. Even today, when I choose to think about it, which is almost never, I can't find an explanation.

During the 8 years I lived in Alba's house, I'd visit my mother's house every couple of years. I never asked to go. I guess Alba felt it was the proper thing, for me to see my mother occasionally. She would send me on a horse, with Homero or someone else. I'd sit behind Homero and hold onto his waist. (Alba didn't know what a good horse rider I was.)

My life as a maid wasn't unhappy. I wanted love, especially the love of a father. I guess living in a household with a father figure gave me some comfort, even though he wasn't home all the time because he was a military man.

I was a very inquisitive and physical girl. I was always jumping fences, or digging or chatting with the town's "ladies of the night" and asking about their jobs. They'd hire me to wash their clothes and I'd use the coins they gave me to buy delicious homemade ice cream. My relationship with Alba was, let's say, normal.

My role was clear: I had to do my chores and obey and take very good care of the kids.

She tended to be overprotective of me, which is why this one occasion is so strange.

I was 12 or 13 years old and a late bloomer. I was so skinny. I had no breasts to speak of and I hadn't gotten my period yet. But every month I suffered excruciating pains in my lower abdomen. I stayed in bed and couldn't go to school or do my work. So Alba sent me to the doctor.

There was only one doctor in Cabrera. Normally he had a nurse with him in the office, Dona Filia. But on the day of my appointment, she wasn't there. It was just me and the doctor, a young man.

"Take off your clothes," he said.

I pulled my flimsy little dress over my head but left my panties on. I hugged myself and waited for him to return to the small examining room.

"I told you to take off everything."

I didn't want to remove my panties in front of him. I started to shake and cry.

"Child, what's your problem? I need to examine you. You need to undress."

Finally I did as I was told. He pressed on my abdomen, looked down my throat, checked my legs (I don't know why).

"Are you menstruating?"

I blushed. "No."

He handed me a prescription. "Take this medicine. And try to eat a little more. You're too skinny." With that, he left the examining room and I stepped back into my underwear and dress.

Once I was back outside in the sun, with the familiar smell of flowers and horses and the ocean, I felt anger rising in me. Alba should have protected me. It's not right to send a girl to see a doctor all by herself. Even though he didn't violate me, he was a man and he saw me naked.

When I got back to Alba's house I handed her the prescription. "Dona Filia wasn't there."

Alba studied the prescription.

"You shouldn't have sent me there alone." I continued. "I had to take off my clothes."

"Of course you had to take off your clothes, child."

"But I shouldn't have to do that...by myself."

"Stop being ridiculous. You're lucky that I sent you to the doctor in the first place."

She had a point. But I still believe that it wasn't right to send a teenaged girl in to see a male doctor by herself.

(V)
Mama

(V)

Mama

I went to Nagua to meet Esperanza, my sister who I hadn't seen for 8 years.

We were practically strangers. On the bus, I tried to imagine what she would look like. I couldn't. Would she recognize me? Would she be good to me? Before I knew it, Rafael, the driver, was telling me to get out. "This is Nagua. Good luck."

I had no address. I was told just to wait. As soon as I stepped down from the bus, I saw this beautiful young woman walking towards me. A busy street separated us and I stood frozen in place while she waited for a break in the traffic. *Could that gorgeous woman really be my sister, or were my eyes playing tricks on me?* Finally the woman ran across the street. As soon as she got close to me, I recognized her. The same playful eyes, the same wide smile. It was her. We hugged and kissed. She smelled familiar and unfamiliar at the same time. She held me out at arm's length to take me in with her eyes, and then she wrapped me in her arms again. I was so happy.

Esperanza welcomed me to the small home she shared with her lover. Life was a little scary for me there. I didn't trust her lover. He owned a motorcycle and whenever he needed to run an errand, he said he needed me to help him. "I have to buy cheese," he told Esperanza one afternoon. "I need your sister to help me carry it."

I didn't want to go but I didn't want to refuse him or my sister. So I climbed onto his motorcycle behind him and put my hands lightly on his waist. He tore down the street and leaned into the turn at the corner. I waited when he went into the store.

When he returned with his small package of cheese wrapped in paper he told me, "It's time you learned to drive the bike. Then if something happens to me, you can do the errands and take care of your sister."

"I don't know. I don't really—"

"Come on, I am a good teacher. Do you think I'm not a good teacher? I promise I'll take good care of you."

I slid to the front of the bike and he pressed his body against mine.

He had me take the motorbike outside of town, on winding farm roads.

"Go faster," he'd yell into my ear. "Faster!"

I gripped the handlebars and concentrated on the bumpy road. He started feeling me up and touching my tiny breasts. I tried to shake him off but the whole bike shimmied. I was terrified. "Faster," he repeated, breathing into my ear. "Go faster."

Finally he directed me back into town and I slowed us down. My ears were ringing and my body felt like it wasn't my own anymore. "Don't tell your sister that I'm teaching you to ride," he told me. "I don't want her to worry."

"But—"

"If you tell her, she is going to fight with me. She won't understand. I'll have to tell her to leave. And you too. You'll both have to leave."

That shut me up. My sister had taken me in and I didn't want to do anything to hurt her. I didn't want to be the reason she would break up with this man, even though he was a bad man.

What a strange situation. His small house by the sea was in such a stunning location. At night, I'd listen to the waves crashing against the shore. I'd listen to the gulls in the morning. But it wasn't a home. No one spoke to each other: not Esperanza and her lover or Esperanza and me. The air always felt tense or scary, I couldn't tell which.

After her love fondled my chest a second time, I decided to take my chances and refuse to go with him to run his errands. I was ready when one morning Esperanza said,

"Doris, go with Luis…" (I just remembered his name!) "…he needs to pick up some things in Matancita."

"I'm sorry," I said, just as I had rehearsed in my head. "I don't want to go with him."

She looked up at me with her big beautiful eyes. "But why not?"

Why not? I hadn't rehearsed that one. "Because… because I'm afraid of the motorcycle." My response hung in the air.

"OK," she finally said.

After that day, Luis stopped talking to me. Then Esperanza and her lover had a fight. I don't know what the fight was about, but Esperanza and I ended up leaving the house in Nagua and going to the Capital.

Esperanza knew my mother's address in the Capital. Mama lived in a two-room shack behind another house. One room served as the living room and kitchen and the other room served as the bedroom. When Esperanza and I arrived, seven people were already living there: Mama, her lover Tonito, my grandfather who had reappeared, my sister Felicia, my older brother Manases, and my younger brothers Rafael and Fredy. When we arrived, it was just so strange. No emotions, no hugs. Maybe that's why today I always love to give hugs. My siblings and I didn't have the chance to grow up together as a family. We never connected as such. Our connection as a family happened as adults. So when we met again, we were like strangers to each other. Felicia, my sweet younger sister, looked at me without saying a word. Finally I just said, "Hola." It wasn't until we were adults that we really got to know each other and love each other like sisters. Now I talk to her three times a day and cannot imagine my life without her.

Between Esperanza, Felicia, and myself, I think my childhood experiences were the most stable. I don't want to go into detail because it is not my story to tell, but I am sad to report that both Felicia and Esperanza endured so much abuse during their childhood and young adulthood. When we were older, Felicia confided in me. I couldn't believe the horror stories she told me. On the outside, Felicia seems happy and easy going, but in her heart she is sad. Only the two of us know why. I want to take her pain from her, to help her carry it. I adore her and I want to protect her. Today she is a loving and devoted mother, grandmother, wife, and sister. Out of all of us, she is the one who took care of our mother during her final years.

For the last ten years of her life, Mama suffered from Alzheimer's. Felicia lived close to her in the Capital and took care of her, always with patience and love. But no matter how much Felicia did for our mother, Mama treated her roughly and without love. I suspect that it was an emotional issue between my mother and Felicia.

When my father passed away, Felicia was just a few weeks old. Maybe Mama resented or rejected Felicia because she came to this world when Papa left it. This is just my own reasoning. I am just trying to find reasons for my mother's behavior towards my sister. Thanks to my sister Felicia, my mother and two younger siblings were able to relocate to New York. Felicia was the first one of us three sisters to obtain her legal status. Therefore, she is the one that helped the family.

I got to know my other siblings as adults as well. My older sister Esperanza is a very good person, but has diverse sensibilities. Her life has been even more traumatizing than mine. I am close to my brothers as well, but two of them I love the more, and like as people.

They are all, except one, married to wonderful women. Some of my sisters-in-law are really sisters. I have love and respect for them. Even the ones that divorced my brothers are still very close to my heart. All my nephews and nieces are very special to me. I admire and respect these young men and women. I am so proud of them as people, as parents, and as family. It is a source of happiness for me to see them taking care of their children and their families. At family gatherings, I see all the smiling faces, the devoted parents, the happy and loved children, and ahhh, it is Heaven to me. How grateful I am for them.

My sister Esperanza (Piran)

My sister Esperanza (Piran), is generous and strong. Her life has been troubled and painful. Starting with that crazy Nenena and the disastrous marriage she forced on Piran. She went through a lot of painful and abusive situations and relationships. My poor sister still seems to me like that little girl, lost in a beautiful woman's body.

After that encounter in Nagua, Piran became my "guardian." She was there for me every time I needed her. And I needed her so many times. She became a mother at a very young age. The father never cared to help her or her baby. This baby, Norma, stayed with my mother until Piran could find some stability in her life. Norma is a loving, smart, and beautiful woman. And just like my sister, she is strong and generous. She is married to a good man, and has four beautiful and smart daughters. During the multiple pregnancies and babies, Norma struggled to be a mother, while also pursuing her own education. She did a very good job at both. Norma is my first born niece, and I love her very dearly. After Norma, my sister had two more kids, Gisel and Hector. I love them so much. When I look at them, I don't see niece and nephew, I see my own kids. After Gisel was born, Piran was able to get their legal status in the USA and then bring over her daughter Norma.

When Piran finally found peace in her personal life, she became ill. She was diagnosed with epilepsy. She gets seizures and loses consciousness. She isn't strong physically any longer, but her willfulness is there. Now I try to be there for her. Even though she has a person at home to help her, she insists on doing things on her own. One day she was home alone and decided to cook. She wasn't allowed to do that, but she did. Well, in the middle of cooking, she had a seizure and lost consciousness.

She left her hand inside the frying pan. She lost four of her fingers and went through excruciating skin grafts. But she is still cooking.

Well, going back to my mother's shack in the Capital was a rough transition. During the day I crawled under one of the 4 little beds. It was dusty and cool, and I guess I felt safe there. I don't know what I was thinking. I wasn't happy. I wasn't sad. Just numb.

I learned that my mother had followed her boyfriend to the Capital and it was a big, big mistake. But he wanted to go there and my mother followed. Here, in the Capital, my family was really, really hungry. In the city, we had no fruit trees, no neighbor farms to steal mangos, sweet potatoes, yucca or bananas. In the Capital there was just dust and raw poverty.

The dwellings pressed so close to each other in the Capital. A few feet from us lived a single mother with her young girl. She sold charcoal to the neighborhood, for cooking. Her business created a lot of dark dust. This dust covered every surface in our little house, no matter how often we cleaned it. On the other side lived a young couple. The husband peddled plantains and vegetables

on a tricycle, with a straw basket in front. I don't imagine
he made a ton of money with this business, but he made
enough to eat every day. And every day his wife, Juanita,
would take the "concon" (rice that sticks to the bottom of
the pot), add a bit of sauce from her meat and her beans,
and give it to us. Around 1:00 PM each day, she'd call to
my mother across from the concrete wall separating our
houses and hand over this awaited dish. Mama divided
the rice into 9 portions. Many days, this was to be the
only food we would eat. I have never forgotten this good
woman and her generosity.

Then there is my older brother Mario. He got himself
a girlfriend and she helped him get into the police force.
Fefita was young, beautiful and very flirtatious. I think
she loved my brother, but because of his poverty and
her own, she also saw other men. One of the other
boyfriends was a young military man. He used to visit
her at Mama's humble place.

One day, as usual, I was hiding under one of the
little beds. Fefita yelled, "Doris, go get water. I have to
take a shower."

I didn't want to do this for her. But I did as I was told, no questions asked.

I crawled out from under the bed, angry and full of dust, all in my clothes and my hair. I walked by her and this man, took the large containers and headed to the place where the whole neighborhood got their water.

"Doris, stop. My friend wants to meet you."

I turned around and looked at them. Then, without saying anything I left the house. I didn't care about her or her friend.

But after that day, every time this military man came over to visit Fefita, he found an excuse to talk to me. Mario told us that this man helped him get into the police force. Well, that was nice. A couple of times after that, I said hello to him, but only hello. I wasn't interested in him. And because I knew he was Fefita's "friend," I didn't like him.

Around this time, I got a job working as a nanny, for a lady who lived in the nice part of the city, in the historic colonial center. I had never been there before, with its old Spanish architecture and cobblestoned streets. I met this lady because she knew a friend of my older half-brother, Felix. Remember him? At this point Felix had become a lawyer, gotten married and had a son. We never saw him. But he did introduce me to this lady who knew a lady who gave me a job.

The woman I worked for lived on the second floor of one of those very old historic houses on Arzobispo Merino Street. She lived with her teenage daughter and her infant grandson. The lady wanted her daughter to go back to study, and needed a nanny for her grandchild. I was an expert in this business! I enjoyed taking care of this big boy. Soon I moved to this house. The lady used to clean all day long. She was tall, skinny and very white. She cleaned from morning to evening. I think she was a little too much. She gave my monthly wages to Felix's friend, who would give the money to my mother.

My employer used to make me get up at 4:00 AM to go to the market and buy the freshest produce. It was still dark when I left that old house. The streets were empty except for drunken men stumbling home, wild dogs, and me. I was scared to death. And to make things worse, the lady was always dissatisfied with my choice of produce. What did I know about the best and freshest produce? Maybe now I know a thing or two, but back then, no sir.

I woke up at 4:00 and worked until midnight. You see, the daughter waited until her mother went to sleep and then snuck out with me. She took me to this bar where she met her male friends, drank, and smoked. My job was to sit nearby and wait for her. I don't know why she made me go with her. Maybe she was afraid to be out late by herself. I wasn't offered even a glass of water.

My life needed to change. I was always sleepy and worried. One time I went to put the baby to sleep and I fell asleep on top of him. I only woke up because he started to cry. That was so scary. This life style was terrible. I needed a change. I told Felix's friend to take me back to my mother's place.

I only stayed in that cramped house for a few weeks. I wanted to leave, to fly away. I was miserable. My only solace was under the little bed. I have always been a happy person, so I knew something wasn't right.

(VI)

Fresa

(VI)

Fresa

Around this time I found out that my Aunt Fresa had also moved to the Capital. Her place was only about ½ mile away on Duarte Street. I moved in with her and her six children, my dear cousins. They were also very poor. Her husband, Papa Fello, fixed watches and traveled around the Capital, looking for work. When he found watches to fix, we ate. When he didn't, we went hungry. But we managed.

Even though they were so poor, they welcomed me with love and tenderness. Fresa, my mother's sister, has always been like a second mother to me and my siblings. After my dear father left us, Fresa was the first person to show me affection.

One day I was crying because I had a terrible toothache. She took me by the hand and we walked to the neighborhood dentist. She held my hand and comforted me when the dentist drilled my tooth. She was protecting me, like a mother should. I felt happy and sad at the same time. Tears started streaming down my face. It wasn't the pain in my tooth. How could I tell her that it was her love and tenderness that made me cry?

A few months after I moved in with my Tia Fresa, my mother came to "take me home." She and Tonito planned to move to El Cumajon, near Nagua. Of course, I didn't want to go with her. I imagine she was sad. But I couldn't understand why out of nowhere, she wanted me with her. It is so sad for me now to think of her, leaving my aunt's house feeling rejected by her daughter, but there was no connection between us, none whatsoever.

One day, Tia Fresa told me that my sister Esperanza was living in a nice neighborhood in the Capital. A married man had taken her as a lover and provided her with a nice apartment. This married man was Armando. He was very good to her, and in the long run, he was very good to me and my family as well. The fact that he was married didn't bother us. When you're poor, there's not much time for reflecting on such details.

At home I helped with the cooking and cleaning. Fresa's oldest daughter Nery and I did most of the work. Esperanza gave Fresa some money to support all of us. With my sister's help and my aunt's good intentions and love, Nery and I were able to go to a commercial institute in the afternoons to study something (I don't remember what). Probably something like typing, filing, and shorthand. That was common then. It was a magical time for me. I felt accepted and protected by a family, and I got to go to school. I always loved school.

Well, as the saying goes, all things – good and bad – must come to an end. After some time, I felt the need to help with this household that had welcomed me with open arms and where I felt loved and accepted. The situation at my aunt was serious. There were too many mouths to feed and only one person struggling on a daily basis to provide for us. I figured, if I could get a job, I could help them also.

A friend of my aunt needed a baby sitter. This lady's household was very rich, compared to ours. She and her husband both had good paying jobs. People used to gossip that they were undercover agents for the current government. I never knew.

Well, I came in highly recommended, after all, since I had 9 or 10 years of experience as a babysitter. The family consisted of two teenaged daughters, from her previous marriage, plus the couple's two children, a 7 year old boy, and the baby, who was 3 years old. My job was to take care of the baby, and to walk and pick up the older boy to and from school. This job was very easy.

At nights I shared a room and bed with the younger of the daughters, Madelene. She was a nice and quiet girl. And you could feel that she was good, so I felt comfortable with her. After two or so weeks, one night I woke up in the middle of the night to feel a man in front of our bed, touching my belly. He just touched my belly. I froze, I was afraid to make a movement.

Well, now I am scared, thinking what to do. Who could it be? In the dark, I couldn't see his face. The only man in the house was the husband. He was usually very quiet and never spoke to me. The first time I prayed it was a dream, but it wasn't. The next time I realized it was real. And not only real, it was the lady's husband. When he noticed that I was awake, he walked away towards their bedroom.

I needed to make a move. I needed to tell someone. I figure, if he is touching my belly, he may be doing the same to the girls. I told Madelene. She believed me, and told me that she didn't trust him at all. (I hoped he wasn't molesting her.) I needed to leave, I couldn't continue there. Madelene told her mother and begged me not to leave.

Carla, that is her name, believed me also. She told me to please help her expose him. She had a plan. The following day was Friday. They went to a family birthday party. We were supposed to pretend that we were asleep. They came home around 2 AM. She went to bed right away, pretending to be drunk. After a while, he approached our bed and proceeded to lift the mosquito net covering us. His hands started to feel for my belly, I wanted to scream. But at that instant, Carla turned on the lights, and got him right there, in front our bed and his arms inside the mosquito net. He couldn't even get up, he was paralyzed. She started to hit him all over. I jumped from the bed, I was afraid he was going to kill all of us. I ran to the nearest window and opened it, to jump out. I was not trying to kill myself, it was a first floor level, but to get out of this house. Everyone woke up and there was screaming and cursing throughout the house. The poor younger kids were running around and screaming. I only knew I needed to get out. Carla ran after me and forced me inside the house. He took his car keys and left the house.

That night no one went to bed again. I felt so, so terrible. I felt responsible for this mess and couldn't stop crying like a mad person. Carla took me by her side, she hugged me and told me that I have nothing to feel responsible for, I was the victim, she said. Wow, a good woman. She told me that she was going to separate from him, not only because of this incident, but because she didn't care about him any longer. She said that that he had changed so much and was always hiding his money from her. She suspected him of infidelities, but tried to stay, so that the two younger kids had a father at home. I asked her what about help with money to feed the family? To me that was so important. She told me not to worry, because financially, she could manage on her own.

Well, I told Carla that even if he left, I needed to go home. (Which home though, I didn't have a home?) I didn't want to go back to Tia Fresa, they didn't need another mouth to feed. Also, I promised Carla that I wouldn't tell anyone about the incident at her place. I kept my promise until now.

The following morning I sent message to Tia Fresa that I needed to contact my sister Esperanza. I was crying but couldn't tell her why. I told her I was feeling sad, for no reason.

(VII)

Piran & Armando

(VII)

Piran & Armando

Soon after arriving in the Capital, Piran moved out of Mama's tiny house. She moved in with a friend. This friend introduced her to some other friends, one of which was Armando. Ah, I forgot to mention some other things. When I was living at my aunt's house, I met this boy my age named Pedro. His mom was the neighborhood school teacher. Pedro had a father and a mother. I liked that. Well, he was my "boyfriend," but just in name. There was never any hanky-panky between us.

At the time, Piran was living with Armando in a second floor apartment in a good neighborhood. I moved in with them. It was so lovely there. Piran and I thought it was perfect. But Armando thought it was too small for the three of us, so he rented a 3- bedroom house in another neighborhood to be able to accommodate me. Soon Piran's little girl, Norma, came to live with us too. This sweet little girl was and has always been like a daughter to me. When she came to live with us, it was a sweet feeling. I played with Norma and my sister was very loving toward the both of us. She bought us new clothes and shoes and we had a refrigerator and plenty of food. I felt like I was living in Paradise.

Piran also sent me to school, another commercial institute. Here I met my dear friend Yliada. She lived near us and I liked her right away. She invited me to her house. I met her mother (no father) and three brothers. One of her brothers fell in love with me. I told him I had a boyfriend, my friend Pedro. But now, my boyfriend and I couldn't see each other much because I lived far away from him. One day I told my sweet Pedro that I liked another boy, just like that. I broke his heart, I imagine. It wasn't easy to say this to him; he was so nice and gentle. And I liked him a little also. I guess since I liked my new girlfriend and wanted to please her, I said yes to her brother. Yliada and I continued going to school together and her brother would carry my notebooks. Yes, just like in the old romantic novelas that Dominicana and I used to read.

My life seemed stable for a while. I was a normal teenager, doing normal teenager things. I went to the movies, for evening walks, played with my sweet little niece. Then the revolution happened.

My parents,
Ramon Pereyra de la Cruz and
Justa Martinez Eusebio

With my sons, Nelson and Julio

With my sisters and brothers.
Front row: Felicia, me and Esperanza.
Back Row: Frey, Rafael, Manasas and Mario.

My husband Richard, with our children, Karen,
Nelson and Julio, on our wedding day.

**Dominicana, Nuris, Maritza
Santos, Migdalia and me.**

**Top: Emerida, Marina and Charo.
Bottom: Loa and me.**

Sitting: Luis, Migdalia, Loa, Dona Vida.
Standing: Diego, Zoila, Maritza Santos,
Arnaldo, Gilda, Nuris, me, Sergio, Tato, Luis
Aristedes, Asuncion, Yova and Baltazar.

**Nuris, Maritza Santos, Asuncion, me,
Dominicana, Sergio and Migdalia.**

My grandson, Dorian

My grandson, Eric

My granddaughter, Lila

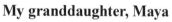

My granddaughter, Maya

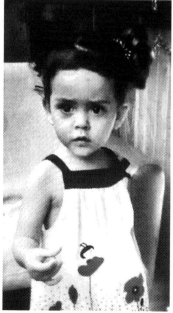

My grandson, Noah

My granddaughters, Justice and Juniper

Dorian

**Juniper
&
Justice**

Maya

Lila

Standing: Justice & Noah
Sitting: Juniper & Lila

Maya & Eric

Lila & Noah

(VIII)

The Revolution of 1965

(VIII)

The Revolution of 1965

In April, 1965 the senior military, backed by the United States, overthrew our first freely elected president, Juan Bosch. The military was divided. One group supported the coup, the other group supported the people. The United States didn't want Bosch. They called him a threat to "democracy," because he wasn't a dictator. Strange, I know.

The Capital was under a strict curfew. Gunfire rang out at all hours. Airplanes roared overhead and dropped bombs. The supporters of democracy and Juan Bosch were winning. Then the US sent in the Marines. Once the US Marines arrived, there was a short cease fire. During the cease fire, Piran sent me and Norma to Mama's house in El Cumajon, Nagua, where she thought we'd be safer.

We had no address, just the name of the village, so I told the driver to let me know when he was passing this village. He did. But there was no entrance to the village, no road or path. Me, being a resourceful (almost) 18 years old woman, decided to take my little charge, Norma, and our bags, and go under the wire fence of a large farm and just start walking. It was daylight and my only fear was that we would find some aggressive cows or dogs. We kept on walking until we saw some houses. At every house I asked, "Do you know Dona Justa?" No one knew her.

I was getting tired, but not my little girl. No, she was and is a very strong cookie. She was jumping around, picking wild flowers. She never complained, even though in some areas, we walked through grass taller than her. I held her hand, and she wanted to run free, but I told her no. I needed to hold onto her so I could keep her safe from the angry animals.

It started getting dark and I was scared. We saw a poor-looking house and once again I walked up to ask if anyone knew Dona Justa. If they didn't I was going to ask if we could spend the night. We walked up to the house and a woman was sweeping the front entrance. It was Mama.

Yes, here was Mama with her boyfriend Tonito, Felicia, Manases, Rafael and Fredy. I was so relieved. This time everyone seemed happy to see us. This house was small and poorly made. Many years later, Piran's husband Armando expanded the house for her. (Yes, Armando divorced his wife and married Piran.)

Tonito had a job, and my mother did laundry and ironed for some policemen in town. One of these policemen always looked at me with interest. I had first met him in the Capital. I liked him a bit but I wasn't really interested in a relationship. Plus, he reminded me of the dusty, ugly little place where we used to live in the Capital.

My mother washed the uniforms of another young police officer, Ramon Paulino. He started to court me. He was so handsome. He asked my mother's permission to visit the house and talk to me. My mother agreed. But just to do that.

One day I had another terrible toothache. I went to see the dentist. The town dentist was, surprise, Don Turin. Yes, the same man that was once married to my crazy Aunt Nenena. They had divorced a long time ago, no surprise there. On my way back from the dentist, I ran into Ramon. He asked me to get on his motorcycle. I did. He talked and talked. He said he had asked my mother for my hand but she said no. He told me he couldn't understand why she didn't like him. She knew his mother and siblings. Well, as you must remember, I was almost 18 years old, physically, but emotionally, maybe 11 or 12. And I behaved as such.

"Don't go home tonight," he said. "You can stay at my aunt's house in Nagua but we'll pretend like we stayed together." This way, he explained, my honor would be destroyed and my mother would have to let me marry him.

"Okay," I agreed.

I stayed with his aunt in Nagua. My poor brother Manases spent the night frantically searching for me. He walked all over town, through the parks, the farms, everywhere. My family thought something terrible happened to me. Even now when I think about my poor brother looking for me, it breaks my heart. How insensitive and cruel of me.

The next morning Ramon went to my mother's house. "Doris stayed with me last night. Now you will give me her hand in marriage."

"I'd rather see her in a coffin than married to you," my mother responded. Wow, she was tough.

We didn't get married, but I had to stay with him. I was disgraced. That was so crazy. I wasn't in love with this young man, I don't think I even knew then what love was. But I stayed. And I used to cry whenever he wasn't around. I really didn't want to stay with him and I think he knew it. He took me to live with his mother in a very remote village. I didn't have any money, nor any ideas or knowledge of my surroundings. I was still in that state of mind where I just did as I was told.

His mother was nice but she didn't know what to do with me because I was crying all the time. Meanwhile Ramon requested a transfer to another town, Sanchez. He brought me with him. Wow, that was no fun at all.

On top of everything, he told me that I was supposed to do his laundry. He had humongous uniforms that needed hand-washing and precise ironing. I hated that work. I also had to stay by myself when he was stationed elsewhere. I feared the dark and I couldn't have a night light because there was no electricity. We had small gas lamps, but we couldn't use them except in emergencies. This is what he told me.

We had nothing in common. He would come home expecting to find warm food on the table, clean ironed clothes, and a willing woman. I stayed at this place for 3 weeks. But each day I was planning how to escape. My days were long, and I was tired of doing these things for him. As soon as he left in the mornings, I cried. When I cooked, I cried. When I washed his uniforms, I cried. When he touched me, I cried. This was killing me.

I became friendly with the lady who lived next door. She was a single mother with 3 kids. I told her that if she gave me the money necessary to pay for my car fare from Sanchez to La Capital, she could take all of our furniture. (By this time, Mama had moved back to the Capital, so I needed to get there). She happily agreed. I told her she had to keep it a secret and hide everything from Ramon, because, he could take it from her. "No problem," she said.

As soon as Ramon went to work the next morning, the neighbor came with a car to take me back to my mother's house. She wasn't angry at me. She even told me I was welcome in her home. That was so nice of her. Especially because, unknown to me, I returned to her house pregnant and with some sort of venereal disease.

During my pregnancy, my mother and I started to form a bond. I didn't know I was pregnant or had a disease, but my mother recognized the signs. She saw my hips and my breasts getting bigger. She told me that my panties were stained and smelly. She sent me to the public hospital. They put me on a bed, with the doors open, and my legs open. They burned something on my genitals. There were no curtains on this room, so anyone passing by could see me.

By this time, the revolution has passed. The country was at peace again. Esperanza's husband Armando came to take Mama and all of us to a small place he had built next to their house. He was the most generous man. He was always happy, always ready for a good time. He wanted everyone around him to be happy. Whatever he had, he shared with us and treated my sister like a queen. On the weekends, he would take us on trips: to the countryside, the rivers, or the beach, My sister would fight with him sometimes because he came home late. But I never saw him mistreat her.

(IX)

Santo Domingo

(IX)

Santo Domingo

We settled into our new place in the Capital. We were now seven: me, Mama, her father, Tonito, Felicia, Rafael, and Fredy. Manases and Mario were both working and helped all of us a little, but Armando was our main source of support. He even paid the doctor to deliver my baby, and every month he bought the formula and whatever we needed. I will always remember him with gratitude and love. Yes, I loved him because he was one of the few men that treated me with respect, like a real brother.

During my pregnancy I'd sit behind our house under a large caoba tree and talk with the ladies that lived on the other side of our yard. They worked at night and they left their children alone. I checked on these kids for them. During the day, three of these ladies each gave me a plate of food. I loved eating their food. I didn't need it. Thanks to Armando we all had enough to eat.

But nevertheless, since I was eating for two, I happily ate whatever they gave me. I think their job was "the night life." Every evening when they left the house to go to work, they looked glamorous. They wore lots of makeup and short-shorts or miniskirts. They smelled of strong, sweet perfume. I was glad to look after their children while they were working. The ladies were so very good and gentle with me. They reminded me of the young ladies in Cabrera who paid me to do their laundry.

On December 24, 1966, for the first time, we celebrated Christmas and had enough for everyone to eat. We shared an entire roasted pig, with lots of vegetables, sweet rice with raisins, baked sweet potatoes, grapes and apples. We were happy, and full, and peaceful. Then, around 9:30 PM, my contractions started. My big-headed son was born 2½ hours later. He was so gorgeous, with a pink face, black hair, and huge brown eyes. He was almost 10 pounds, boy, really big! (I guess since I ate for two, he got some of my food.)

Nelson.

When I gave birth to Nelson, I was so happy. I didn't know what it meant to be a mother. I was 20 years old. But emotionally, maybe 15.

Over time, we became a terrible burden for Armando. Financially he couldn't continue supporting all of us. He and Piran started fighting all the time. We lived in fear that he would leave her. My sister told us that his businesses were doing very poorly, that he was scared for the future of all of us.

After Nelson turned one, I tried to look for a job in the city. But I didn't have any preparation, not even high school. Ramon came to see his son and told me to get back together with him. He wanted us to get married, but I refused. I kept on looking for work. Since I didn't have money to pay for the bus, I'd look for work on foot. I walked everywhere. When I was lucky enough to get an interview, a man (always a man) sitting behind a big desk would ask me what experience I had. None. What skills did I have? None, but I was smart and a fast learner. Their responses were all the same, "If you give me a little, once in a while, we could negotiate some arrangement." They all kept a large desk and a large sofa in their offices. Their large desks were to allow someone to go underneath to service them, and it was the same story with the sofa. I would just give them a look and walk away.

Meanwhile Ramon continued insisting that we get married. Now we had a son, why not? I hated him. He had given me that smelly disease, and I remembered the cooking and washing and ironing and cleaning. But Manases wasn't making much money at all. And Mario had gotten married. So, something had to give.

Ramon never paid a cent to support his son. When Nelson was a baby he got very, very sick. He had a high fever, was vomiting and had diarrhea. His life was in danger. He needed intravenous fluids, but we didn't have money to take him to a safe doctor. By this time, we couldn't ask Armando to help us. He and Piran had split up and he had moved to Puerto Rico.

I needed to get help for my baby. It was a very hot summer day. I took my *cabezon* and walked 3 kilometers to get to the center of the city. I knew the name of a good pediatrician in private practice. He agreed to treat him. Nelson stayed as an inpatient there for 5 days and recovered. At that time, they made you pay your bill before they released your child.

While Nelson was in the private hospital, I walked to the Palacio Nacional. I asked where Ramon was stationed. They looked up the information and allowed me to call him from one of their phones. I explained the situation to him and asked for money to pay the bill.

"Will you move in with me?" he asked.

"This isn't about us. This is about Nelson."

"If you won't move in with me, then let the doctor keep your son."

I walked back to the doctor's office sobbing. "I don't have the money to pay the bill," I told the doctor. "But if you release Nelson to my mother I will go to your house right now and work as a maid until I've paid the bill."

The doctor was a kind man but he didn't say anything.

"Or you could send me to jail. But please don't keep my baby."

"Senorita, I will speak with my partners. I can't make any decisions on my own, but I will ask them to forgive your debt."

He spoke to them, and I brought Nelson home in my arms later that day.

(I forgot to mention that when Ramon found out I had sold his furniture and ran away, he got on his motorcycle and sped to my mother's house. My mother insulted him and he left and never came back. I didn't see him again until my precious son Nelson was born.)

When Nelson was about a year and a half old, Fresa's daughter Nery got married. In the morning of the wedding, I left my mother's house with flowers we had cut from the front garden. My mother gave me 10 cents to pay for the car ride to Fresa's house. I stopped the car and got in. I asked the driver if he was going my way, he said yes. A few minutes later the car stopped and picked up another passenger. I didn't look up.

"Driver, take us to the Malecon." It was Ramon. He pressed his body against mine in the back of the car.

"No, don't!" I protested.

But Ramon was in his military uniform and he was a man. The driver took us to the Malecon, the road by the ocean. By this time I was crying.

When the driver stopped the car, Ramon gripped my arm. "She's my wife," he told the driver.

I held onto the car door and begged the driver not to leave me with Ramon. But Ramon pulled my hands away from the door and dragged me away.

The Malecon was nearly deserted. It was 7:30 in the morning.

"I'm going to kill you, you bitch."

I expected him to reach for his revolver at any moment. "You just keep walking with me until we find a real lonely place, because I'm going to kill you and throw your body to the sharks."

I sobbed as he pulled me along, holding my arm and my shoulder.

We walked and walked like this, by the sea. Finally he said, "I haven't killed you yet because I haven't found a place lonely enough." Maybe he didn't intend to kill me. I don't know. Every time I looked at his face though, I saw tears, so I knew he was really serious about his intentions.

Still holding onto me, he hailed a public car. "San Cristobal," he told the driver. San Cristobal? That was an hour from the Capital. No one spoke a word during the journey. The driver took us to a giant sugar cane plantation. One of Ramon's uncles lived there.

At that moment I had an idea. "Ramon, I've changed my mind. If you go back to the Capital and get our son, I'll marry you."

"I knew you'd come around," he said. He led me into a small room on the second floor. "Tio, you're responsible for her. Don't let her leave this room. If she's not here when I get back, you'll have to answer to me." Ramon looked terrifying in his full military uniform, with his weapon hanging by his hip.

The uncle nodded his head. He looked over at me and I could tell he didn't have the fierceness to hold me hostage. He knew my mother. As soon as Ramon left, I told the uncle, "I'm leaving."

"You can't leave. Ramon said—"

I walked to the balcony and began to climb over the railing. "Try and stop me and I'll jump."

He sighed. I guess he saw the complication of the situation and decided to do nothing. I walked downstairs and out through the front door. I ran down the plantation path until I got to the road. I waited for a vehicle to come. After a few minutes, I saw a big truck transporting sugar cane. I got in the middle of the road, so that the driver couldn't miss me. He stopped.

"Please, please give me a ride to town. I don't have any money but it's an emergency."

This man was so nice. I couldn't reach the seat in the truck. He got out and lifted me up. The truck driver dropped me off in a park in a nearby town, where there were cars headed to the Capital. My plan was to get to Mama before Ramon and take my son and go into hiding.

But first I had to get to Mama's house. I approached the driver of a new red car. "I'll pay you whatever you want if you drive me to the Capital and promise not to pick up any other passengers.

He looked at me from head to toe. "Show me your money."

"I don't have any, but my family is waiting for me and they can pay you whatever you want. I promise." I was lying, of course, but I hoped they'd have something to give him. He was a working man and couldn't afford to drive people around for free.

After a moment he cocked his head, motioning for me to get into the back seat of his car. He kept his word and drove straight to Mama's house without stopping. We arrived around 3:30 in the afternoon. A crowd of family and neighbors had gathered. When I hadn't shown up at Nery's wedding, word spread and people got worried about me. I jumped out of the car and told Mama what happened. She took up a collection with the neighbors and gave the driver a pile of money. I don't know how much he got from them. I hope it was enough.

I took Nelson and a full bottle of milk. A neighbor hid me in her closet. Ramon arrived 30 minutes later. He had lost time because first he stopped at his aunt's house. He asked her to go with him to my mother's house, so that she could distract Mama while he took Nelson. Well, his aunt refused to do that.

When Ramon arrived by himself, my mother asked, "Where is Doris?"

"I don't know. How am I supposed to know?"

"Where is she? I swear—" Mama said.

"Why are you asking me?"

Mama, all 4 foot 10 inches of her, began to punch Ramon, her fists flying at his chest. "You know why I'm asking you, you bad, bad man. She beat you here and she has her son. You'll never see them again. Get used to it."

He didn't strike her back. He didn't raise his voice. "Tell your daughter that as long as my gun has a bullet in it, she better not let me see her. I swear to God I will kill her. I will shoot her in front of you if I have to."

When he said that, my mother lost her strength and had to be helped down to a bench. My grandfather also got sick from the fear of his threats.

I don't understand why Mario, who was a policeman at the time, didn't denounce Ramon or do something to protect me. Mario must have had a really good reason. Maybe Mama never told him about this, just to protect him. She didn't want a confrontation between these two military men. That was probably the reason.

After Ramon left Mama's house, he hunted for me and Nelson in all the houses in the neighborhood. He barged in and searched all of the rooms. He stormed into the room where Nelson and I were hiding. But Nelson was sleeping in my arms and we hid behind a pile of sheets and blankets, inside a large closet, so he didn't find us.

The next day my mother sent me to Santiago, where my half-brother Feliz was living. He was married and had a child, my dear nephew, Alberto. From there, I called Yliada and told her about my situation. She told me that her brother had moved to New York but that he always asked about me.

"Yliada, I'm really scared. My son and I need to leave the country."

"Don't worry. I'm sure my brother will help you. He'd do anything for you."

She told her brother Julio about my situation and he helped me escape. But he told me that I needed to come alone. It was too dangerous to bring a child on this adventure. He sent me money to get a passport. He had a plan.

The day I returned from Santiago to my mother's house, I left my precious son with her. I needed to go to save my life, to get a job, and to support my son and help my family.

(X)

New York

(X)

New York

"Tell me the plan again, to make sure you remember it."

"First I go to the airport with my passport. I go to the counter to pick up my ticket."

"Yes. I bought you a ticket. It's in your name. Where is the ticket to?"

"Venezuela. But it has a stop in New York. Also Leda will be with me. "Leda was a family friend my age who wanted to take a chance and leave Santo Domingo also.

"In New York I get off the plane and I look for a sign." I paused. "What if this doesn't work?"

"Don't worry. If you follow my instructions and stay calm you'll be fine. You look for a big sign that says 'E-X-I-T.' Go outside and look for a taxi. Then what? Do you have the paper I sent you?"

I held a creased piece of paper in my shaking hand. "Yes. I give that paper to the driver and he will take me to your apartment."

"That's right. Then give the driver the dollars I sent you when he drops you off. And you understand that you couldn't do this with a baby, right my love?"

I bit my lip to keep from crying into the phone.

I woke up in the predawn hours on the day of the journey. I slipped out of my mother's house without saying goodbye to her or to my beautiful sleeping boy. Leda and I met at the airport. I was grateful for that, because she was more mature and confident than I was at that time. She guided me and gave me strength to take the risk. I was so sure we were going to be turned back home.

But everything worked, as they say, according to plan. By mid-afternoon I was sitting in Dona Evangelina's apartment in Washington Heights. It was taken for granted that I was Julio's girlfriend and as such I was received. Again, I was with a man I hardly knew and did not love. But we became a couple. His family was very loving and good to me. Julio got a furnished room where we lived for a while. On this occasion, as on many others, I did what was expected of me. So for 10 years I was his wife. I got pregnant and we got married. I did this because I was so grateful to him. He saved my life.

The day after I arrived, Julio took me to see Piran and Armando. They had reconciled and moved to New York. They had a baby together, Gisel, another niece that is very close to my heart. Norma was back in Santo Domingo with Mama and Nelson.

Two days later, Julio gave me some money and instructions to go down to 14th Street and buy a job. Yes, at that time, it was a common thing to buy a job. The placement office sent me to a factory downtown. I have no recollection of the area or the address, even though I worked there for about two years.

The owner of the factory was a middle-aged Jewish man. He interviewed me through an interpreter.

"Are you a fast learner?"

"Very fast."

"How old are you?"

"Twenty two."

He pulled at his beard and looked me up and down. I was skinny and didn't look my age. "I'm going to need some proof of that."

"Yes sir." I took the subway back up to Dona Evangelina's, got my passport, and returned to the factory. I have no idea how I did all of this. Aside from my passport, I had no papers. But the factory owner didn't care about that. Just my age.

I loved working at the factory. I learned to make women's house dresses and winter hats. The nice Spanish ladies helped me a lot. They gave me lunch every day and taught me some words in English. I remember a middle-aged Italian lady that also treated me so kindly. Her husband had died and she had no children. I was happy. I was working and sending money to my mother. Now life was looking good.

After work, I'd take English classes at a local high school. On Saturdays, I went to a commercial institute on 42nd Street, where I learned how to be a key punch operator. I wanted to be prepared.

Potito

My second son, Julio, was born on March 15, 1971. He was born premature, at 7 months. He was small and so cute and sweet. (He is still cute and sweet.) After 2 long years, I was finally able to get my legal status in the United States and bring my dear Nelson home with me. The day I arrived home with my two kids was the happiest day for me. I was able to care and cook for both of them.

My son Julio, my sweet Poto, has always been very close to me. Nelson and I are close too, but Julio is more demonstrative. With Nelson, you feel the love, you see it in his actions. They both are amazing human beings. I like them as people. I am sad that I didn't have them with me all of the time. They went back and forth between Santo Domingo and New York. I knew I was missing so much of their childhoods, but I had pressure to leave them with Mama and I was afraid I wouldn't be able to manage caring for them in New York, all by myself. Mama meant well, she just wanted the best for them. Somehow, she felt that only she could do it.

My Flaco (Nelson) was a very skinny and strong little boy. When men looked at me on the street, he wanted to fight them. "Mami, I'm skinny and small, but I can fight any big man. I can protect you." He still protects me. Both of my sons do. Being a mother and then a grandmother have been my greatest accomplishments.

Now I felt my life was complete. I'd go to work, come home, and cook for my family. Not that I relished the cooking part, but because I wanted to feed them, it was a happy task. Feeding my children meant everything to me. I never wanted them to know hunger like I had when I was a girl.

But then my husband Julio started to drink. He'd get drunk, fight with me, and abuse Nelson. One night, he got close to me and I could smell the alcohol on his breath. "Why do you hug and kiss Nelson so much? Huh? You missing his father? Is that it?" Julio was a jealous man. He had emotional problems that he carried from his childhood. There was tragedy in his life, but not something that I feel free to talk about.

Julio would still go to work every day, but wouldn't come home until very late. And very drunk. My life became a nightmare. I tried to keep him calm, so that he wouldn't hurt Nelson or me. It was tough.

By now, my mother and siblings had also moved to New York. Felicia married a man who helped her get papers for herself, Mama, and our younger brothers, Rafael and Frey. They were all living in Yonkers.

I needed to get away from Julio, but this time I didn't want to go to my mother for help. I spoke with Ramirez, Dominicana's husband. He was a big shot at a company in the Capital. He was also a good friend.

(XI)

Santo Domingo

Two Glorious Years

(XI)

Santo Domingo
Two Glorious Years

I told Julio I was taking the children to Santo Domingo for a two week vacation. He didn't object. Ramirez got me a job at his company and I shared a house with a woman named Mireya and her son. Her son was a year older than Potito. I had left Nelson with Mama in Yonkers, because I wanted him to finish out the school year. Six months later, my brother Mario brought Nelson to me in Santo Domingo. When I had both of my boys with me, I rented a bigger house. Every morning, we'd leave the house together. I'd walk my boys to the school bus, then I'd board the company bus that took me to work. Life was hard. My salary wasn't enough to support the three of us. But our life was a dream to me.

But after a few months, my husband Julio reappeared. "Let me make it up to you," he pleaded. "I've stopped drinking. You can't do this on your own. I can get a job here and help you out. I can move in and pay the rent." After a while, he wore me down and he began staying with us. At first it was all right. But before long, he began drinking again.

One day I came home and Julio and Potito were in the yard. Meanwhile, Nelson was in the house crying. Julio had mistreated Nelson again. That was the final straw for me. I know that Julio was trying to stay sober and be nice to both kids. But he was weak. Remember, he was a traumatized man. His childhood had been a nightmare. For that reason and because he had helped me when I needed it so badly, I had patience with him. But my patience had ended. I needed to protect my children, especially Nelson.

It hurt me to leave my job in Santo Domingo. I had made amazing friends. Friends I am still close to today, including Mirian, Mireya, and Esperanza (Pera). We'd go out after work sometimes. We'd go to an outdoor restaurant and eat tostones and salchichas and drink ice cold Presidente beer. We laughed and laughed together.

Even though the pay wasn't good, the job was a pleasure. I worked as a key punch operator in Ramirez's office. Every day at 10 AM, and 3 PM, a young lady walked around the office with a dainty tray filled with small cups of black and aromatic cafecito. I've never cared for coffee, but I'd take a cup just to hold it in my hands and pretend to drink. And I did taste a sip or two.

The company bus took us to work in the morning, home for lunch, and back home again in the evenings. I loved coming home and serving dinner to my boys. Many nights we did our bedtime routine in the dark, because the electricity wasn't stable. But we didn't care. We had each other.

I needed to keep my boys safe. I started to plan. I quit my beloved job, borrowed money for plane tickets, and waited. One morning I told Julio I was taking the boys to get their vaccinations. Instead, Nelson, Potito and I headed straight to the airport. To avoid suspicion, I didn't take anything with us. No luggage, no clothing, no books. At the time, Nelson was ten and Potito was six.

(XII)

New York, Again

My Children, My Family

(XII)

New York, Again
My Children, My Family

When we arrived in New York in the winter of 1977, we moved in with Victoria. Victoria is one of Mario's ex-wives and a good friend of mine. She welcomed us and we felt at home. Felicia was also living with Victoria. She had left her husband and was hiding, just like me. That evening I called Julio and told him that we were in New York and that we weren't coming back, ever. He was angry, I guess.

The next day I asked Dona Juana, a friend of Victoria's, to watch my kids and Felicia's kids so we could look for work. My mother was living in Yonkers, but we couldn't bring the kids there because Felicia's husband or my husband could find us. Felicia and I both quickly found work. But the work was far from Victoria's: two hours each way. Meanwhile our kids weren't happy with Dona Juana. She was too strict and dry. That was a problem. We decided to wait for the next school year to start and for things to calm down with our husbands. Then we could take our kids to Yonkers, where Mama could watch them.

We registered the kids at the school near Mama's in Yonkers. The plan was for them to stay with Mama during the week. On Fridays we would pick them up after work, and take them to Victoria's in Brooklyn, until Sunday afternoon. Felicia and I were terrified every time we went to Yonkers. A lot of Dominican people lived in Mama's neighborhood. If anyone recognized us, they could tell one of our husbands. But we didn't get caught. After a year, once things had calmed down, Felicia and I planned to finally move to Yonkers, to be with Mama and the kids.

"I'm not staying here," Mama declared. "I'm going back to Santo Domingo."

"But Mama, we are ready to move here to Yonkers and be with you and our children."

"No. This is not a good environment for children. The boys need a strong hand. And this is no place to raise a girl."

"Then we'll find a place for all of us in Brooklyn," I said.

"I'm done with this terrible city. I'm done living inside these four walls. You stay here, work, and let me take the kids with me."

Felicia had worked as hard as I had to stay with her beautiful children, Carlos and Jackie. We pleaded with Mama, but her mind was made up. She told us that if we didn't let her grandchildren go with her, she'd be lonely. She told us that she needed money from us to support her in Santo Domingo and if we had our children with us in New York there wouldn't be enough left over to send to her.

She convinced us and we allowed our kids to go with her back to the Dominican Republic. Our hearts ached for them. And they missed us too. A year and half later, Mama decided to move back to New York. We were thrilled because now we could be together again.

Meanwhile, Felicia and I had to get a larger apartment and prepare to receive them. We moved to a large apartment in Brooklyn. It was a nice place. The kids went to school. I took them to the Y to learn to swim, to museums, to the park, to restaurants (only cheap ones, as money was still tight). Our younger brother Fredy also lived with us at this time. He was going to college but couldn't get a job, so we were helping him too. He got angry with us because we had boyfriends. We were still in the process of growing up.

"You go out too much," he would tell us. "You should stay home and do the cooking and the housework, so that it doesn't all fall on Mama's shoulders." He was right. Mama also got tired of this arrangement and decided, once again, to move back to Santo Domingo.

'That's fine if that's what you want, Mama. But this time our children stay with us." Felicia and I did the math. We thought we could keep the apartment if we rented out one of the rooms. But we wouldn't have enough left over to send money to Mama.

Mama didn't fight us that day. She strategized. The following week, our hearts sank when we saw that she had invited our older brother Mario to come up from Santo Domingo to talk to us. By this time he was a high ranking officer in the police force. He carried himself like an important man.

"Look girls, you both know you can't protect your children here. They aren't going to listen to you and you'd be putting them in danger." He ran his finger over the rim of his cafecito. "You're grown women now, so act like it. You're being selfish and childish. Do what's best for your children."

I felt the heat rising in my cheeks but I didn't say anything.

"I can protect them. No one comes close to anyone in the family in the Capital. I can't protect them in New York. You know this is true. Mama knows this is true. That's why she told me to come and talk some sense into both of you."

At the time, neither Felicia nor I had the maturity to fight and keep our kids with us. We didn't trust ourselves to know what was right for our children. We let Mario and Mama convince us that they knew best.

We didn't know what it meant to be parents. I feel so much pain when I imagine that part of their childhoods, being shuttled back and forth all the time. We moved them constantly, changed their schools all the time, and nothing was stable. It's amazing that they turned out the way they did, such good and caring people. I know they bear the scars of not having their parents with them all the time. Children, I am so, so sorry.

Not long after Mama took our kids back to Santo Domingo, Felicia lost her job. She couldn't find another one. She decided to move back to the Dominican Republic. She was going to live with Mama and the children and look for work there. She met a very good policeman, Fernando, and married him. He has been a gift to all of us. He takes care of Felicia. He has been a father figure to so many of my nieces and nephews.

I stayed in New York with the intention of returning later. To save money, I rented a single room and continued sending money to Santo Domingo. Within a year, I secured a good job at the New York City Transit Authority, based in the World Trade Center. This job paid good money and had good medical and dental coverage. I got an apartment in Brooklyn. Then, my sons came over to live with me, this time, mercifully, for good.

Before Mama moved back that time, we helped her get US citizenship. Felicia found work and I didn't have to send as much money any more. My two younger brothers, Rafael and Fredy, had married and had their own children. I love these nieces and nephews very much. Some of them are physically far away, but always in my heart.

After a while, we moved to a small studio apartment, also in Brooklyn, in the Downtown area. This came in handy, when my job moved to 25 Chapel Street, also in Downtown Brooklyn. Mama, once again, returned to New York and moved in with us in our tiny studio apartment. It was okay; we were used to small quarters. Nelson got a job and told me that he was thinking of moving in with a friend. He was a good kid. He got a job and was doing well at school.

The apartment was a happy, busy, and crowded place. I welcomed all of Nelson and Julio's friends. They knew they could eat whatever was in the refrigerator. I was so happy to be able to stock it with food and feed them! (My cousin Juan, the superintendent of the building, often helped load the refrigerator, with groceries he bought for us.) We always had one or two nephews staying with us.

Once again, Mama went back to Santo Domingo. She had the spirit of a wanderer. She couldn't stay in one place for long. In retrospect, I wonder if she was suffering from the early stages of Alzheimer's.

I decided to go back to school and earn my college degree. I had always been interested in psychology. I registered at the Brooklyn campus of Long Island University, which was a block and a half from my apartment. It was convenient. I had to work hard, harder than most. Those years were some of the happiest of my life. I had my kids, my job, school, and friends. I also started piano lessons. I love the piano. I also started painting. I discovered that to paint was (and is) my greatest passion. I felt so complete, and so in charge of my life. It was the first time I truly felt that way. It was 1986; I was 40.

In 1991, I graduated from college with a BA in Psychology. It was such a great accomplishment for me. I worked like a horse for five years to keep my grades up. To get into college I had to take the GED. I started college ignorant in so many subjects: English grammar rules, statistics, algebra, calculus. I learned it all because I wanted to do it. I wanted to do it for myself and I wanted to show my kids that with hard work, you can achieve your dreams.

My sons grew into men. In 1990, Nelson had a male roommate, before moving in with a girlfriend, who was a bit crazy. Then he got an apartment by himself. He graduated from college and got a job at NYC Transit. Julio started college and was doing well. He had a girlfriend that caused us lots of problems. Julio and this girlfriend lived in the studio because her father had thrown her out. Felicia's daughter Jackie was living with us as well. She has always been very attached to me. (And I to her.) She is like my own daughter. I only had two boys, but I have such a loving relationship with all my nieces and nephews that they are like my children too.

Jackie was living with us and I wanted to guide her without being too harsh with her. I loved her and I knew she thought I was the cool aunt and that I was easy to get along with. That's true, but I also wanted her to do something with her life, something more than being someone's girlfriend or wife. I had a talk with her. She cried.

"I know you're sad today," I told her. But tomorrow promise me this: figure out what you want to do. You can go to school or you can find work." But she did it her way and she got married. I feel sorry for her and a little guilty. She wasn't happy at my place, and I couldn't help her.

Julio's girlfriend was extremely disrespectful and abusive to all of us. One day, she insulted Jackie. Jackie told me I had to throw her out. I talked with Julio and he begged me to let her stay. "Mami, she has nowhere to go. She'll be on the streets." I couldn't throw out Julio's girlfriend.

At this time, I also started talking with this man from work, Richard. He was a manager in another department. He invited me to lunch one day and I told him I would love to go, but I couldn't. I had just finished a very troubled relationship and was afraid to go out with another man. He understood and never invited me again. I wanted to stay free for a while. Up until this point, all my romantic relationships had been a string of disasters. And I was really tired of them all.

One year later, I applied to Hunter College for a Masters in Social Work. I needed a letter from someone at work. So I asked Richard. He wrote a very nice letter for me. Later on, he asked me out again. This time I said yes. He seemed so gentle and honest. We started dating, but just dating. Soon things evolved and we got serious.

When he asked me to marry him, I said yes. But I wanted us to each keep our own apartments. He had been on his own for 17 years. And I was used to being on my own too. Three months later, in August, 1992, we got married. Coincidentally, our wedding was the same day as Jackie's. (Jackie, my dear, I'm sorry I wasn't able to make life easier for you.)

We had a very small wedding at the courthouse in Queens. The only attendees were Karen, Julio, and Nelson. A very informal wedding, I liked that way, so did Richard.

Karen is Richard's sweet and beautiful daughter. The day of our wedding, she told me, "I am the daughter you never had." That was profound and I loved her then; I adore her now. She is an amazing woman. I like her as a person and I love her as a daughter. I am grateful to Susan, her mom. I am grateful to her for sharing her daughter with me. If I had my own daughter, I don't think I could love her more.

Karen met and married a young and very good man, Paul. They have two children. My two adorable grandchildren., Noah and Lila. They live far away from us, but we visit and they visit us. Paul has a lovely family in Toronto. We love them and feel that they are our family too. Whenever I visit them in Seattle, I feel so good. I feel loved and accepted. My grandchildren call me *abuela,* and I love that. The older boy is so tender and loving, and extremely smart. The girl, what an interesting character this little girl has! From early on, you could see that this little girl would be a very strong and loving woman. When they visit us, she sleeps in my room with me. We talk a lot before going to sleep. Our conversations are very interesting, to say the least.

When Lila was six years old, during one of my visits to Seattle, she told me, "The people in New York are lucky."

"Why?" I asked her.

"Because they have you." With that line, you can tell a lot about this precious girl.

Karen is very family-oriented. Every time they visit us, they go out of their way to visit Julio and Nelson, so that the children can get to know each other.

My sweet Jackie married this young man, a good person. But neither of them was emotionally ready to be married. They had a precious son that we love very much. But the relationship didn't work. They were both in the process of growing up – just like me. I was still growing up. Slowly but surely. Later on, Jackie remarried and had a daughter. This daughter is beautiful and looks just like her. Her husband is a good, hardworking man. Jackie went back to college, got her degree, and then got a very good job at a hospital in Queens. She is a sweet and loving mother. She had matured and has learned to love and value herself. I am very proud of her. And she loves me like a second mother.

My sons were happy with my relationship with Richard. They accepted him. Nelson was already working and living on his own. My dear Poto was still living with me. He still needed the connection with my home. And that was completely acceptable to me. But I pushed him to do something with himself. And the fact that his girlfriend was living with us was very inconvenient. She was troubled.

After Richard and I got married, I continued living in my apartment with Julio and his girlfriend. Richard lived in his apartment in Queens. That was the agreement.

I used to go and stay with Richard on the weekends. One Saturday night, around 11:30 PM, Julio called. "Mom, can you come over and help me get this crazy woman out of here?"

Richard and I raced over. When we arrived, the police were there. My heart was beating out of my chest. The apartment was a mess. The TV was on the floor, and papers were strewn everywhere. She was yelling at the police officers. Julio was almost in tears. One of the policeman took me aside. He told me to get her out of my place. He said she was trouble. Yes, I knew that.

Richard and I drove her to her father's house somewhere in the Bronx. The father had thrown her out of the apartment, due to her behavior. But that night, we brought her back to him.

That night Richard told me, "You and Julio have to move in with me. And your parrot, Cuca. We'll rent your apartment." I agreed. But it wasn't easy. Richard is a very organized and disciplined person, me and Julio, not so much. And Cuca was a crazy bird with a big mouth. Richard was set in his ways and we disrupted all of his routines. I started to have acid reflux and to grind my teeth at night. I had no peace.

During the first year we lived together, we had so many talks. Some were peaceful. Some weren't peaceful.

Meanwhile, Julio wasn't working or going to school. I was worried about him, but I knew my son. He wasn't ready to make a move. But Richard told me we had to scare him into doing something. "If he doesn't go to school or get a job, we need to tell him he has to move out."

I refused.

I also wanted Julio to move forward in his life, but I knew that emotionally he needed time. Richard was stricter than me. At the same time, Richard is very generous.

Julio wanted a personal computer. "Get a job," I told him. "Save up for half the cost of the computer. I'll cover the other half." He got a little job, but was never able to save a penny. Why, I don't know.

But Richard went ahead and bought him a computer. "Just pay me back, a little at a time." And Julio did pay him back, a little at a time.

And then there was my dear, dear Cuca. When she talked and looked at me with those little brown eyes, I saw love in them. Yes, we communicated. Well, when we moved to Richard's apartment, she changed. She fell in love with Richard. She started to bite me every time I approached her. Before that, she would sit on my shoulder and stay there while I cooked or painted. Now she attacked me. She also started to pluck her feathers. She did so much damage to herself. We took her to the vet. He diagnosed her with "emotional problems."

The vet suggested we take her to a pet shop and see if they would let her live there for a while. Supposedly, she was too lonely during the day. We did that and we'd visit her everyday on our way home after work. She seemed happy. I loved her so much. But it seems that one of the employees also fell in love with her too. One day we stopped by to see her and she wasn't there. The employee disappeared and so did Cuca. The owner of the store claimed he had no responsibility to us, that he was just doing us a favor. This was over 25 years ago, and I still have dreams about my lovely Cuca. I hope wherever she is, whoever took her, that they love her as much as I did.

When he was ready, Julio got a better job and a better girlfriend. This girlfriend, Jennifer, is his wife today. She is a very good wife and a very good mother. At the beginning they had their ups and downs, but at the moment, they have a very solid relationship. They have two girls, my adorable granddaughters, Justice and Juniper. We go to them on Tuesdays. Richard brings them bagels that they adore. (Their dog, Julius, adores the bagels, too.) Richard helps them with homework and in return, they feed him candies.

I help with whatever I can, sometimes even cooking white rice for them. That is the only food they allow me to make. Remember, I am a terrible cook. Many times, I feel tired and my body hurts all over, but once I get there and see their smiling and loving faces, everything feels right. Juniper is loving and warm. She reminds me so much of her dad when he was a child. She loves to hug and to be hugged. Justice is a sweet and adorable young woman. I look at her and feel such a tender warmth inside. She is mature for her age, very self-possessed and calm. Justice disciplined Juni and made sure that Juni did her homework and attended to her things when she was very young. Now, Juni is very responsible and takes care of her school work and other activities, without any guidance from Justice. Even though they always do things together, Juni looks up to Justice for the important decisions.

Jennifer works very hard to support the family. They decided to sacrifice for a couple of years, so that Julio could go back to school and finish his college degree in fine arts. Now he has finished school and graduated with honors. They rented a studio where Julio works on his art and does jobs on commission. I feel comfortable in their home. Richard comes with me to their house, takes the dog, Julius, for a walk and brings all of them bagels. I do manipulate the girls into eating more fruits and vegetables. I teach them some Spanish words and make sure they drink enough liquids. And even though they don't like this, I try to control their sugar intake. I love folding their clothes. Julio does the laundry and I fold. Folding clothes is the only house work I enjoy.

Julio is a very good husband and father, and a loving son. He loves his girls and would do anything for them. He continues painting and drawing. The walls are full of their art. Jennifer always supports and motivates Julio to work on his art.

Unfortunately, as of this writing, my two precious sons aren't talking to each other, but I have faith that someday things will be different. I won't go into details of this painful situation, I just hope. They are both good men and neither one has done any harm to the other. They are both amazing good sons. I am grateful for that. They love and respect me.

Nelson had a short relationship with a young German woman. She got pregnant and had a son. Yes, my first beautiful grandson, Dorian. It's sad, because for many of his childhood years, we had very little contact with him, because he lived in Germany with his mom. The first time I met this kid, I started to cry. Dorian was the same age as Nelson was the first time I left him with Mama. Wow, my cabezon. The relationship with Dorian's mother has been difficult. She kept us from being a regular part of Dorian's life. She had a child with another man, and we wanted to love him also, but she did some dishonest stuff that created even more distance.

When Dorian was 16 years old, she allowed him to come to the United States by himself. She had a boyfriend that didn't like him. Originally, the plan was that he would stay with Nelson for a year. Instead, he moved here permanently. Dorian is happy, doing great in college and is an amazingly good person. He is a good kid and calls his mother every week.

Later on, Nelson had a girlfriend named Anya. For a couple of months they broke up and he started dating a young Swedish woman. Well, the young woman got pregnant and went back to Sweden without telling Nelson. That is what Nelson told me.

Meanwhile, Nelson and Anya got back together and eventually got married. They had a daughter,

Maya. She is precious and so much like Nelson. Things got complicated because before this little girl was conceived, Nelson found out that he had a son in Sweden. Yes, another precious and loving son, Eric. Another grandson for me. Anya had a problem with this. She didn't believe that Eric was conceived while she and Nelson weren't together. And she didn't want Nelson to be a part of Eric's life. But Nelson needed and wanted to be part of this boy's life.

When Maya was two years old, Nelson and Anya divorced. That pained me because I knew that Nelson wanted to make this relationship work. He wanted to be part of his daughter's life. However, he wasn't happy in the relationship. Still, he wanted to stay. He was an unhappy husband, but a happy and loving dad.

Well, as of this writing, Nelson lives in a beautiful apartment. He cares for his oldest son on a permanent basis. He cares for his daughter on weekends. And on Thursdays, he picks her up from school and stays with her until the mother gets home. The Swedish family are very good people. I love them and recently Nelson took me with him to Sweden to see them. We had an amazing time; they are so loving and treated us very well. I am so glad they are Eric's family; he comes from good people. They come over and visit. Nelson loves all his children very much. He learned to cook and prides himself on making dishes for his kids. On Sundays, when Maya is with him, Richard and I come over to help and to see his children. I admire and respect him. Nelson is a good person and a great Dad.

Recently, I started to pick up Maya from school one day a week. It is a pleasure for me. We talk and play. She is always happy to tell stories and play. But homework is a different story. I need to put on my serious face. Maya is very loving towards her Dad. She loves him and looks out for him. She has a very sensitive nature and loves all kinds of bugs. Whenever she sees a bug, she wants to take it home and make a bed for it. After a while I had to stop coming over to pick her up from school. They live in a building without an elevator. Their apartment is on the 4th floor. It's very painful for me to walk up and down stairs, due to back complications.

(XIII)

Re-Encounter with My Childhood

(XIII)

Re-Encounter with My Childhood

All through the years, during my struggles to survive and my many relationships and ups and downs, I never forgot my childhood friends. Once in a while I would go back, in my mind, and see them. I wondered what had their lives been like? Did any of them have to go through similar situations like me? Were they alive, were they happy, did they have children? I mainly thought about Dominicana and the other 10 'Fosforitos.' What were they doing? Were some of them still in Cabrera?

But it wasn't too often that I consciously thought about them. My life was filled with my own personal struggles and experiences. I was extremely busy and emotionally unstable, making wrong decisions, one after another, and learning and growing, oh so slowly.

Many years later (I think I was already in New York), I found out that Dominicana had been looking for me. Remember, when I left Cabrera, I didn't say good-by to anyone, not even to her. My leaving Cabrera was a surprise for me, too. I wondered what they all thought when they found out that I was gone? No one knew where I went. Alba probably just told them that I went to live with my own family. Up to that time, I believe they all thought I was related to Alba or to her husband. So my disappearance was a mystery to them.

I was 28 or 30 years old when I was able to reconnect with Dominicana and Maritza Martinez. By then, I had already run away with one guy (Nelson's father) and married another guy (the one that helped me come over to the United States, who was Julio's father), before divorcing him (this was a lot, indeed).

Maritza was living in Queens, New York and Dominicana was living in Santo Domingo, Dominican Republic. Maritza was married and had a daughter. We reconnected again, and we even shared an apartment (for me to save money) during one of my mother's trips to DR with my children. But somehow we lost touch again. Later on, Maritza moved to another state and we lost touch yet again.

Dominicana was married also. During one of my trips back to the Dominican Republic, my friend Dominicana reconnected me with Migdalia, another dear friend. It was really good to see her. I always liked her a lot. Sometimes, when I visited the Dominican Republic, Dominicana would invite Migdalia and the three of us, or I should say, the two of them (my reputation as a bad cook, is well known) would make some delicious meals that we all enjoyed so very much. Other times, we would go out and eat. But it was always a happy occasion to meet up with both of them.

Still, it was mainly Dominicana that I stayed in touch with and visited more often. When my kids were with Mama in the DR and I visited them, I would always make a side trip to see Dominicana. More often, she would come over, with her husband, Alejandro (also an old friend), to see me, at my mother's house. We would talk about the others. *"Where were they?"* I would ask Dominicana. She knew about some of them, but she had lost contact with others. (Unbeknownst to me, some of them also lived in the United States.) We also talked about Cabrera. I would tell Dominicana that I wanted (once my kids were grown up and independent) to move back to Cabrera, to build a little house in the outskirts of Cabrera and live there peacefully, raising chickens and growing my own vegetables. In other words, I wanted to go back to my roots. On those occasions, she would tell me, "Doris, you are living in a dream, our Cabrera is not what it used to be when we were kids. It has changed so much, the people are not the same, too many streets, too many stores, too much of everything." Nevertheless, I kept my ideal of Cabrera. I wanted to go back, some day. We also spoke about each and every one of our closest childhood friends, the 'Fosforitos' (just wondering about them all).

Well, the years went by. My kids were already young men, smart, handsome and good people (this is a mother talking). I was working, had gone back to finish my education, was in a good place, emotionally. At my last job, I met and married a very good man, Richard. He is a good person. I admire and respect him because he is such a good son to his elderly mother. His mother and I have become good friends. Sometimes I forget she is my mother-in-law, because there is no tension. Richard is an amazing dad to his adorable daughter, Karen. This was the second marriage for both of us. The beginning was rocky, but we overcame everything.

During one of my conversations with my dear friend Dominicana, she told me she had encountered, by chance, one of our other dear friends, Maritza Santos, at a funeral home. I was extremely happy. I asked if I could have her phone number. I called the same day and she was as excited as I was when we spoke. She seemed like the same sweet young girl I knew more than 54 years before. She was living at the time in Puerto Plata. She told me that she had lived in New York for over 40 years and had now retired to live near her children. I promised that whenever I visited the Dominican Republic, I would stop over to see her.

In the Summer of 2016, I traveled with my sister Felicia and her husband Fernando to Santo Domingo. They were planning on building a small apartment in the Capital. My brother-in-law, who is such a good person, told me not to worry, he would drive me over to Puerto Plata to see my friend. We rented a car and drove over there. Maritza waited for us at the entrance of the city; she wanted to make sure we didn't get lost.

When we saw each other, it was just beautiful. She was so welcoming, sweet and generous with us. She hadn't changed; she had the same sweet and loving personality. She took us to her house, a beautiful, large house in Puerto Plata and gave us homemade cookies. These cookies were intended for her son, who was traveling that day to New York, but had forgotten them (so we gladly took them). Then she took us for a tour of the city. The old Victorian neighborhood maintained all of these wonderful antique structures, which we found very interesting. She also took us to this bakery that made the most delicious bread, which was so, so good. I forgot to tell you that my friend Maritza is part Jewish. (Her grandfather is Jewish.) Finally, we went to a restaurant and had a nice lunch. We talked and talked, and promised to stay in touch forever. I asked her about the others.

She told me that there were some friends living in New York. One of these girls was Charo Ramon. I went to look for her on Facebook, under the name Ana Ramon (that was her real name). I only knew her as Charo. She also told me about our friend Loa. I looked for her on Facebook under her real name, Dinora Eusebio. You see, when we were growing up, we only new each other by our nicknames. As adults now, they were known by their real *"grown up"* names. Dominicana also told me that she had heard from Zoila, who was also living in New York. I returned from the Dominican with this treasury of information. I was going to find them. It was the time to reconnect.

I was able to locate Charo, Loa and Zoila on Facebook. I sent out friend invitations. Charo replied but didn't seem as excited as I was. I invited her for a cup of coffee, hmm, again with not too much enthusiasm from her. I didn't insist for a while. Zoila didn't reply to my FB invitation. I tried Loa, but couldn't locate her. I was disappointed, but didn't give up.

One day I went to visit my dear Alba Rosa. She is one of the Alba's children. (Remember, Alba is my Godmother and the one who raised me). When I left Alba's home, there were only 3 boys. After that, she had 2 more girls.

As adults, we reconnected and showed out love for one another. These girls are amazing, loving and strong women. I respect and admire them. I also reconnected with Alba, as I have real feelings for her. She is different, too. Life and time changes us, sometimes makes us mellow.

I explained to Alba Rosa about my search for my childhood friends. She told me to call Amparo, who is a very nice woman from Cabrera that has always been very close to my Godmother's family. I met her years back and I always liked her. So I called her and she gave me so much information. She told me that our dear Professor Cuchito (from the 8th level) was also living in Brooklyn. She also gave me Loa's phone number and told me that Marina was living here. Marina is another good friend from Cabrera. She is not part of the 'Fosforitos,' but she is an amazing woman, and one of the many that continues – from her adopted country – to help Cabrera and its people. She is the daughter of Filla, remember her? She was Cabrera's nurse, midwife and counselor (a friend to everyone).

When I called Loa, it was like magic. (Loa was the sweet and timid girl that Dominicana and I wrote that "fake" romantic love letter during our last school year.) Well, she had remained sweet and lovely. It was such a wonderful conversation, both of us seemed equally happy. She gave me the phone number to call Cuchito, our old professor. It happens that he had married Loa's sister, Adela. I also found out that we were actually related as a family. We share my mother's side of the family last name. I am so happy to call her my 'cousin.'

The same day I called Cuchito and when he answered the phone, his voice was young and strong, which was amazing. I was expecting to hear the voice of a very old and feeble man. But no, he sounded young. I told him who I was and he remembered me right away, including my nickname. They called me *'meneito,'* because I used to walk so fast all the time and my skirt would dance, from side to side. So, that was the *'little movement.'* I decided right there that I needed to go over and see him and Adela and their children. They have 8 adult children and 17 grandchildren.

I told Dominicana of this great news and she was so happy that she wanted to see him, too. When I complained about not being able to get Zoila and Charo, Dominicana promised to get Zoila's phone number for me. She called her brother, Arnaldo. Finally, I was able to contact Zoila. She was very happy and excited about talking with me, about my plans to go and visit our dear Professor Cuchito. She told me, "Doris, we have to prepare something big, we have to get together, all the 'Fosforitos' residing here in New York."

Zoila is a very capable and resourceful woman. She started the planning, by creating a Chat in WhatsApp, where we could all connect with the others and share our plans and ideas. This was a good way to connect with both the ones living here and the ones in the Dominican Republic. I went back to Facebook and explained to Charo about our plans. This time she was very receptive. And so it started.

There was a daily 'madness' to it all By the end of the week we had Loa, Charo, Zoila and Doris in New York and Dominicana, Maritza Santos, Migdalia, Arnaldo, Rey, Tato, and Sergio in the Dominican Republic all in on the plan. Every day, we'd just talk and plan, talk and plan. Later on, one of Prof. Cuchito's sons, Tony, joined us. We got through to him through Arnaldo, in Cabrera. He provided important information that we needed for our plans. It was going to be a surprise visit, so we needed a connection to his family. We were all on board.

Each day, starting at 6:00 AM, one of the girls (I still call them girls, even though we are all seniors), usually Charo, would start texting and talking, talking about us, about our common history, our lives in Cabrera and after Cabrera. Usually at this hour I was still in bed, but Charo and Loa and Maritza Santos are up early and chatting, chatting. We are so thankful for this new technology that allows us to enjoy this amazing closeness on a daily basis (most importantly, it is free). We were planning our surprise visit to Prof. Cuchito for October, but decided to change to November in order to wait for Arnaldo, who also wanted to be part of this happy event. Each of us has our own, unique specialty. Maritza Santos sent us the most amazing videos, with various topics: life, philosophy, humor, love, friendship, etc. Some of the others also sent some treasuries of thoughts, to make us smile or to just inspire us. They also sent many religious, political, and scenic videos. One item everyone sent was love and prayers.

Our daily Chat was joined by some more of our dear childhood friends, Yova, Nuris, y Asuncion, as well some male friends, Arnaldo, Sergio, and Rey, who are relatives to a few of the girls, and have always been amazing to us. Also Tato, one of my closest male friends from my childhood, joined in. These guys are and have always been there for us. The four of them are gentle, honest and good men. They are extremely generous and caring.

We were all so excited about Arnaldo coming over. We asked him to bring us some of those Dominican treats we missed so much, like Ron Brugal, Tercia, coconut candies and milk and sweet potatoes candies.

During our conversations, all of us, boys and girls, shared our memories, our stories, our love for each other and the promise, a very loving and sincere promise, to never again disconnect – to be there for each other. It was very good to have the male input. They seemed to remember many things that we girls had forgotten. We talked about music, about the old songs of our time. Sometimes we prayed together, as most of us are very religious.

We gave each other electronic hugs and support. During the month of November, the day before our meeting with Professor Cuchito, Maritza Santos' aunt passed away. We all were there for her, sending our words of support and love. Also during this month of November, torrential rains affected our Cabrera, as well as Puerto Plata. Rivers were overflowing and houses and roads in poor neighborhoods and near the rivers were destroyed. There was no loss of human life, but the loss of farms and crops had far-reaching effects on the lives of the residents. Our dear Loa's family was one of these families affected.

At times like these, the men I previously mentioned, Arnald, Tato, Sergio and Rey went into action, helping to rebuild houses and to offer other forms of immediate help to these poor people. They also kept us informed.

We set November 17, 2016 for our surprise visit to our ex-Professor. Zoila, our main organizer, prepared a banner, a plaque and flowers for him and for his wife, Adela. I made red paper hearts with white letters and decorations, representing each one of the Fosforitos. As you remember, this is the name that some of us were known by, when we left Cabrera. My friends Dominicana, Maritza Santos and Migdalia wanted so very much to be here with us, but they couldn't make it. So, we planned to represent them with a red heart and a letter that each one of them had sent, via Chat, to our ex Prof.

We prepared some food to bring over to Cuchito's and we waited excitedly in the lobby, until we all were together. Loa was in charge of getting Professor Cuchito and his wife ready for us, without them knowing all the details. It was necessary to tell him something, as we didn't want to just jump on him, since he is an old man. Adela told him that one or two people from Cabrera were visiting.

The day of the surprise I took a taxi from home. I was carrying too many packages. I was carrying food, the handmade coasters that I made for each one of my friends and for Cuchito's children, the red hearts and other smaller items. I also made some special coasters with the image of a heart on each, with a verse I had once read. It read: *A Friendship does not need the person to be present in order to be maintained and grown, it grows by the magic of knowing that he or she is always carried in your heart.*

You can imagine the excitement. We hadn't seen each other or our ex-professor for over 54 years. I was the first one to arrive and I waited in the lobby, as was agreed upon. I was standing there with my heart racing in my chest, and looking at every woman passing by, to see if it was one of them. Would I be able to recognize any of them?

The first one was Loa, she was supposed to be upstairs with them, but she was running late. We saw each other and we just ran toward each other and hugged a long hug. We couldn't even say anything, we just looked at each other, touched our faces and our hands and laughed. She remains one of the sweetest, gentle people I know. We waited together for the others.

From Catalina...with Love

The next one was Charo, ah, the same, she looks great and hasn't change her bright smile and happy disposition. We got a phone call from Zoila. They were at the train station, waiting for a taxi, because Dona Vida (Zoila and Arnaldo's mom) was there with them. We were so happy to see her also. She was very old, but so very strong and sweet and happy to share this occasion with us. We all loved her so very much, and enjoyed having her there because she is one of the few mothers remaining. We all love her and have adopted her as our mother.

Meanwhile the three of us were there waiting and Adela (Cuchito's wife, Loa's sister and my cousin) arrived. She knew we were going to be there. Loa told her everything about the plan. She approached us, looking with her big eyes and a smile on her face. She came over and hugged me, and said, *"Doris, is this you?"* Ah, it was just raw happiness. She did the same to Charo. Adela looked very well; age hadn't changed her physical appearance much.

She came down because she knew we were carrying food and wanted us to bring it upstairs, to the refrigerator. But the problem was that Cuchito was upstairs and we didn't want him to see us until the others arrived. Adela told me to come up with her and Loa, just to bring the food. She was sure he wouldn't recognize me. I was instructed not to look at him, which was hard. Just go in, drop the food, and walk out. Charo stayed down to wait. When we got to the door, she realized she had forgotten the keys, so we had to ring the bell. He came over to open the door, and as instructed, I didn't look up, just passed by him, put the food down. Loa said hello to him, then proceeded to walk out. She said to me, "Come Juanita, let's go down." I saw him from the side and I wanted so bad to give him a hug. He was looking surprised; he didn't know who this strange woman that came with Loa was. And the woman was rude, she didn't even say hello to him. That is what he told me later on.

We were all looking out, waiting to see our dear Zoila, Arnaldo and Dona Vida. When they arrived, it was just so much happiness. Remember, it had been so many years without knowing anything about each other. We all wanted to hug Dona Vida so much, she is such a sweet lady, always has been. And she treats us all with the same caring smile, just like our own Moms. We were all so excited, all of us, since every day we were able to celebrate our friendship. How is it possible that our feelings for each other remained through the years? Yes, our feelings for each other were awakened after a long, long time.

The group was assembled, orders were given and we marched into our dear Professor Cuchito's apartment. Each one of us was holding a big red heart, made out of cardboard, with some sentiment on it. We were all talking at the same time, he didn't know who to look at, we kept on asking him, "Do you remember me, do you remember me," and he was just looking without saying a word. We hugged him and he sat dawn; he was clearly overwhelmed. We talked amongst one another and with Cuchito's family. They were so loving and grateful that we were there for their father. They had delicious food, drinks and sweets for us. Arnaldo also brought for sweets from the DR. We all drank and danced so much. We all took turns dancing 'merenge' with our Professor Cuchito. At around 5:30 PM, Marina arrived. We had invited her, as we all love her and wanted to see her, as well. She is the same, a loving woman. She brought delicious candy made out of milk and raisins. I sat next to her and we talked a little, but it was impossible to stay in a conversation, as everyone wanted a piece of each other. Around 7:00 PM, we started to prepare to leave. We knew he was tired. We left with the promise to come back. We needed to comeback just to see him again. I wanted to talk to him about our country, our Cabrera and our times. I needed to visit him by myself on another occasion. We left with the promise that this wasn't the last time we would meet. We all wanted to stay connected.

After our encounter with Professor Cuchito, we thought that our daily Chat was going to be over. Not even close. It had been 3 months and we are still going strong. It is such a source of comfort to get up each morning and see our Chat page full of loving wishes, of loving greetings. Each day there is someone or some relative going through a situation, could be sad or happy, but we are sharing each other lives, whatever it is. Chevalier and Emerida also joined our Chat.

We found out that one of our 'Fosforitos,' Maritza Martinez, is going through some family issues and at the moment wouldn't be joining us in our daily Chat. But I spoke with her and she was very happy to hear about our re-encounter and how we are reliving our friendship and love for each other. We are hoping that she will eventually join us. I also found out that she had another child, a son, an adult son.

On November 25, 2016, one of the 20th Century's great men, Fidel Castro, died. This morning one of our dear friends, Arnaldo, took a photo of the news and posted it on our daily Chat. When I read it, I stopped for a moment to see if any of the other friends was going to comment. Remember, we love each other, but that love was born in our childhood. We knew each other as children, adolescents, but not as adults. We are starting to know each other now. So, I didn't know their political or social ideals or preferences. No one commented, so I decided to take a chance. We needed to be honest about ourselves. I needed to be honest and express my real feelings about this great man, and hoped that my friends were going to be, if not approving, at least respectful of my opinion. I wrote: I just read about a great loss. I admired and respected his original ideals: To take some from the ones that had so much, and distribute among the poor, that had nothing. To provide free education and medical care for all. The Cuban people, infrastructure and life style suffered, but it wasn't his fault. It was the fault of the embargo and false propaganda by the United States. Without realizing that the punishment wasn't to Castro, it was to the Cuban people. Or maybe they did realize it, but just didn't care.

Well, I posted and just waited. I was a bit apprehensive. I didn't want to offend any of my friends' sensitivities. My dear friend Maritza Santos was the first one to respond. Her response was just what I was hoping for. I have to quote this in Spanish. : *"Cuba sufrio no por la politica de Fidel Castro, sino por el bloqueo economico de los Estados Unidos. Y aun asi, sobrevivieron."*

This was followed by comments from Arnaldo, Sergio and Charo. Their responses were so similar to mine and Maritza. I really appreciated that. Some of their comments: Two of the greatest men of the 20th Century, Fidel and Mandela. "They were two men to learn from and to imitate." It was just pure joy to read this from my dear friends. I am so proud of them.

It is such a source of happiness for me to have them in my life again. And the beauty of this is that the feeling is mutual. We keep on repeating the same line – We never forgot you and we always wanted to find you. Just an amazing group of friends.

As I said earlier, each morning, the first one to start the conversation is Charo. She gets up super early. Usually by 5:00 AM she is already typing, sending good wishes and prayers and blessings. And she is usually the last one to stop typing at the end of the day. I didn't tell her, but before I go to bed, I lower the volume of my cell phone. I need my beauty sleep. Maritza or Loa follow Charo; they are all early risers. They go to bed late and get up early.

Our lives have changed after our re-encounter. We bring happiness and comfort to each other. We are sisters and brothers. We are so happy, I think, because we bring up and share the happiest of memories: our adolescent years, our childhood mischiefts, our loves and secrets; those days when the only worry was to hide behind a tree to read a novelita romantic, or to go horse riding, or to smoke a cigarette, maybe.

One of our favorites pastimes is to post names of old songs from our times. For example, Nicolas Di Bari/ Guitarra suena mas bajo. Dyango/Si la vieras con mis ojos. Agustin Lara/Noche de Ronda. Marco Antonio Solis/Donde estara mi primavera.

Sergio and Dominicana are the poets of the group. They remember the most profound lyrics. Their choices of songs are so very touching. But Maritza and Charo and Loa also have an immense repertoire of beautiful, romantic songs. Sergio sent us photos of his beautiful wife and kids. Hopefully, we will meet them when we travel to DR.

Our next encounter was planned for July of 2017. We wanted to come over in October, just to stay away from the hot weather, but our friends insisted we come over in July. This is the month they celebrate the *"Cabrerenos Ausentes."* This event is celebrated every year in the Dominican Republic, for the people that were born or raised in Cabrera, but due to circumstances, have moved away. This event has been celebrated for over 40 years. The majority of those who've left do return for this event, which is celebrated the last week of the month of July.

The boys, Arnaldo, Tato, Sergio and Rey, together with Migdalia, Dominicana, Maritza Santos, Nuris, Yova and Asuncion, are planning to receive us. They made certain plans for us, but the main objective is to make us comfortable and happy. We would arrive in the capital, then continue to Cabrera, which is about 3 hours away. We would go to all the places we used to visit as children (rivers, beaches, parks, etc.)

This event takes a lot of preparation from our friends. They had to find a large house that will accommodate all of us, since we want to remain together. We are planning to go one night and roast a pig at the beach, eat and drink and stay there to wait for the sunrise. Charo suggested we cook outdoors, in a stove made up of 3 large rocks (as it was done in the past). We want to eat the food that our parents used to make for us. (The ones lucky enough to have parents.)

We would also go to Dominicana's little house up on a hill in Catalina. This house is precious, surrounded by flowers and fruit trees and all kinds of animals. The view is magnificent, and a constant breeze invites you to stay forever. The daily talk and day dreaming of this event would keep all of us in a constant happy state. We all have the dream of re-living our happy, long gone childhood. Our friends had a lot of plans for us, plans which they were keeping secret. We wouldn't find out until we arrived.

On some days, one of the ladies is absent from our Chat for a whole day. That is not uncommon for some of the ladies or guys, but for some it is rare. Charo and Loa and Zoila and Maritza and myself are always there, even if it is only in the late afternoon. So if one of us stays away for a whole day, the others would be worried. We got very used to hearing from each other every day. The ladies in DR sometimes stay away and we wait patiently. But if more it's than one day, we start to question: Where is so and so, we haven't heard from her or from him? And so on. Our male friends are not always present on a daily basis, but whenever they join in, we are overjoyed. They bring in different topics of conversation, which usually makes all of us happy.

Having more friends come into the chat, as we went along, added even more love and interest to our daily talks. These friends were known to my friends, and remained in touch through the years. I had known them also, but wasn't in touch with them, for no particular reason at all, just geography and life. There is also Leandro, a very dear and good man who is divorced and lives alone in the Capital. He chose not to be a part of our daily Chat, so we worry about him, because he seems to be is leading a lonely life.

One day, Charo told us she was sad. She was driving her car and had a little accident. She didn't get hurt, but the car was left in bad shape. Sometimes she forgets that she should not drive when she drinks!! So, though we don't tell her, we are happy she doesn't drive anymore. (Yes, we were all so happy to hear she had to give up the car.) All we can do is offer her our unconditional love and support. She is very sensitive, with a big and loving heart. We respect and love her. As she is the first one to enter our Chat on most days, we worry about her when she goes absent for a whole day, though we have learned to respect her space. We continued our plans for our group visit to Cabrera.

We finally decided on July 26th for our trip to Cabrera, Dominican Republic. We informed our friends, so that they could proceed with their plans to receive us. I would leave on Sunday July 23rd, as I wanted to be there a couple of days before our reunion, to have some free and special time with my dear friend Dominicana. Zoila left on Monday July 24th and Loa and Charo left on Tuesday, July 25th.

Before that anticipated day, some of us (including me) went through some scary moments or days. We were so, so afraid that we couldn't make it. About 10 days before my departure day, my dear Mother-in-law fell and broke her hip. Mind you, she is a 94-year old woman who weighs just 84 pounds. Well, at the hospital the doctors performed surgery and her leg started the healing process, but it was too much for her weak little body. For two or three days, she couldn't eat or open her eyes. At times she was hallucinating. We were so afraid that we were going to lose her. I was particularly afraid. (God please do not let it happen.) Our God did listen to us. Mom started to eat again, which was not an easy task for her, as she has narrowing of the esophagus and it makes swallowing very difficult. But, she is a trooper. She came around and just 3 days before my scheduled departure, she was transferred to a Rehabilitation center, to regain her physical strength and her lung capacity. I left with a heavy heart. I was sorry to leave Richard alone, but he was predictably generous and encouraged me to go. "Go and enjoy yourself," he said. During my Mother-in-law's hospital stay, her dear granddaughter Karen was in town for a few days. She came over with her husband, Paul and with Noah and Lila, her children. Having Karen with us was a blessing. She helped us so much, both physically and emotionally. She is strong and we needed that strength.

Loa was going through a similar situation. Her sister Adela (Professor Cuchito's wife), was very delicate and in the hospital with heart problems. Loa didn't say anything to us until after Adela came home. Charo had an incident where she went shopping and left her purse at the counter. She lost money and important papers. Ahhhh, but we ultimately did it.

HERE I COME!!!!! Sunday, 7/23/2017.

When I arrived, Leo, a very dear friend of my family, picked me up at the airport and drove me to Dominicana. Our encounter was very emotional. The following day Zoila arrived, but went to her family for that day. On Tuesday, the 25th, Leo went back to the airport to pick up Loa and Charo. Dominicana and I were so filled with anticipation to receive them. Rosi, a very good young woman who comes during the week to help my friend out and keep her company, helped Dominicana make a delicious sancocho for dinner. When Loa and Charo arrived, there were more tears of joy. Charo started to cry and she was clearly overwhelmed. It had been a very long time since she last visited her native country. Before we had time for dinner, though, Zoila, Arnaldo and Tato arrived and it was total madness. Tato is younger than us, maybe 5 years younger, and small in stature, so we all look at him as our sweet little brother. It took a while before we could calm down and start dinner.

That evening, we officially started the party. We enjoyed our dinner, drank and danced and laughed until late at night. Once in a while, one of us would get up, walk over to someone and just hug them, just look into those eyes of our childhood memories. Around 11:00 PM, it was decided that the guys should go home and we all should go to bed. Zoila and I shared a bed. Charo went to the living room and fell asleep on a comfortable sofa. Loa went to her room and waited for Charo, but Charo never came. She decided to stay on the couch. We set up our alarm clocks to wake up at 5:00 AM.

At 6:00 AM, Wednesday, Arnaldo y Leandro arrived. They were going to drive all of us to Cabrera. On the drive to Cabrera, I was in one car with Zoila. We talked so much, sang religious songs and talked about men, relationships and life in general. The 3-hour trip seemed like only 1 hour. We were just enjoying the sweet smell and feel of the air, the green vegetation and the limitless fields of rice. The high and green mountains and the amazing clouds got me to taking photos like a machine. I wanted to capture every single little thing, the cows and horses freely walking in the farms, the man on the donkey carrying his green bananas and sweet potatoes and avocados, or the farmer with his machete cutting down dry grass to prepare the land for new harvest. There was so much land, with green, luscious vegetation on both sides of the road. Even the mountains were colorful. Where man had cut through the mountains to build roads, you could see the heart of the mountains, in red, purple and orange, which was just beautiful.

Throughout the trip, we tried to stay close by. Whenever one car stopped, the others did the same. We wanted to stop on the road and buy food that we had enjoyed in our childhood (mainly, chicharron and fried sweet potatoes and boiled yucca and avocados). We found many of the same foods we used to eat whenever we travelled through these roads, familiar roads, but at the same time changed roads (more modern in so many ways). There were modern toll booths, wider roads, with alerting gadgets and lights. The price of the tolls reflected the modernization costs. But we had instructions not to buy any food, since we were supposed to stay hungry, because Milo was making an amazing breakfast for us. One thing we were allowed to do was drink, yes drink (and not only water).

When we were approaching the entrance to the town, everything looked so strange. We kept on asking questions like, "And where was the house where I grew up?" or "Where was this or that store located." Now, where a house used to be, we could see a store or a bar or a computer lab. Most of all, I couldn't identify the location of Alba's house. Back then, there was a small plantain farm next to the house, but now it's just a street with different beautiful houses.

We arrived at the park, our lovely park, which held so many memories. Even though the park does not look a bit like our old park, still, the sentiment was there. Each new bench, new tree, new decoration was viewed through the eyes of our memories. But there were no more almond trees. When we arrived, there were a lot of people waiting for us. It was an incredible feeling. Hugging familiar and unfamiliar faces, just hugging and laughing. Everyone wanted to welcome the 'Fosforitos.' I was happy to see a fresh coconut vendor on the corner. That was my treat. The younger generation didn't know us, or us them. They were the ones asking, who are they? Our friends explained: They are Cabrera, they are a demonstration of true friendship and love, because these people became friends more than 60 years ago, and remain friends, real friends. They came back here today to celebrate their long lasting friendship.

From the park we went to Milo's. Many people followed us. We arrived at *El Breton*, a beautiful country house where Milo and Luis were waiting for us. This house faced the ocean and was located on an incline, so that the breeze was always a pleasure. Our friends had prepared so many things for our entertainment, with banners, pins, t-shirts, flowers and decorations, all intended to make us feel welcome.

And we did feel very welcomed. A table was set up with a variety of food, more delicious and healthy food from our childhood. There was Yuca, Avocados, eggs, plantains, aullama, (calabaza), Yautia, and others. Also homemade drinks, made from tropical fruits. After some time, when we were able to calm down and started to eat. Milo and Luis were amazing hosts. After breakfast, we danced, exchanged stories and ate a wonderful homemade desert, rice pudding.

We were sitting under a humungous almond tree. There were a lot of ripe almonds, which were so sweet, that I started to eat some. Milo even brought me a tray with a bunch of these almonds, and I ate about 5 of them, while also taking photos of them. Those almonds and almond trees are so rooted in my memories, that eating them was an emotional feast.

When we finally left Milo, we went to *La Bomba*, which is a family bar. Here we continued drinking and dancing. Our main host, Arnaldo, was also our guide, friend, brother, companion and everything under the sun. He kept us moving, from one place to another. He was there for us from morning to night. He lives in the Capital, with his wife and adult children. But at one point, he had to leave us and didn't return until Sunday, the same day that some of us left Cabrera to return to la Capital. His wife is such a good and generous woman; she gave him the freedom to be with us all of that time. We were very grateful to her.

We eventually went home to change clothes. In the evening, we went to the house of our dear Nuris and she had a surprise for us: a party with live music and dinner. She had prepared a variety of foods that she knew we all loved. We danced and (supposedly) had a competition to see which couple would win a prize as the best dancers. I was petrified. If you see my friends dancing, you will really realize what a bad dancer I am (no rhythm whatsoever). My friends, men and women, are all fantastic dancers. I enjoyed just watching them. Well, I just danced one or two dances, and the other time just witnessed their dancing skills. But I was drinking and eating and talking to so many people. I wanted to get drunk, maybe, so I thought, as a way to improve my dancing, but no. I didn't get drunk and I didn't improve anything. After Midnight, it was announced that the dance competition was a draw. They all won. It was just for fun.

After Midnight, we went to our room to sleep. It was a very large room with 2 beds, located on the third floor of a house owned by Nuris' aunt, Dona Iliria, a very good and generous person. For two consecutive days she made sure we came down for breakfast and coffee. We met her daughters and other relatives. Well, we had five women that had to sleep in two beds, so it was decided that Charo and Zoila would share one bed, while Maritza, Loa and myself would share the other, larger bed. We didn't care, we were there to have fun, so not much sleep was needed. Neither Maritza nor Loa liked to sleep in the middle, so I was the chosen one, which was no problem. The three of us slept like little angels.

Every night, Charo would come home later than us, a bit drunk. She would undress, only kept her underwear, and went to the galleria and sat on a rocking chair, where she would fall asleep. Around 5 or 6 in the morning, Charo would come over to the bed and join Zoila, who is a good sleeper. One night, Charo came home especially drunk, so much so that when we tried (with Arnaldo's help) to put her into the bed, the bed collapsed! We all fell to the floor, but Charo didn't notice anything. Two of the legs on one side of the bed broke. So now the bed was tilted to one side. Everynight, Zoila would go to bed with her head leaning toward the upper side of the bed (in a very narrow space), so as to leave enough room for Charo. And every morning when she woke up, there was Charo, sleeping, head down.

During our stay, some of us suffered some injuries. One night I got up to go to the bathroom, on the way back to bed, missed the step leading back to the bedroom and spun around until I finally landed on my back against a desk. I hurt my back, head and arms. Well, with the noise I made when I landed, everyone woke up. They got worried when they saw me in the floor, crying in pain. Originally, when they heard the noise, they thought that Charo was the one on the floor. They helped me up, a little, but I couldn't stand up straight. We didn't know what to do. They all wanted to help me, but how? Loa got some Vick's Vapor Rub to apply on my bruises, but Zoila, who is a Doctor, very seriously, said "How can you think of applying that to the raw skin?" Poor Loa felt bad, but Zoila was right. They managed to take me to bed and I lay down on my side. And since my position in the bed was in the middle, Loa and Maritza, on either side of me, would sit up in bed every 5 minutes or so to see if I was alive. It was so sweet, but I tried not to go to sleep, mainly because my head hurt. I was so sleepy, though, so I thought, in all honesty, "If I die here, tonight, it would be marvelous. Dying so happy, I could care less." (By the next morning I was awake and ready to mambo.)

Thursday morning's agenda was to meet at the park at 10:00 AM. Arnaldo would meet us there, to take us to the next adventure. We got up around 6:30 AM, because we couldn't stay in bed any longer, there was far too much excitement. Every morning, before brushing our teeth, we would sit down in the small galleria. There were 4 big, comfortable black rocking chairs, so we sat there and just talked and spent some time getting to know each other again. One morning, someone knocked at our door and when we opened it; the neighbor from the 2nd floor was standing there. The young woman (whose name I can't remember) was so nice that she prepared a large tray with some dainty

beans and cabbage salad. She had also arranged for some live music for us to dance to. We stayed there for over 5 hours, eating, drinking and dancing. Everyone was drunk, either from alcohol or from happiness. (I think I was drunk from both.) It turned out that even our friends who were in more delicate health than the rest of us (Sunsa, Leopa and Leandro) danced and had a blast. At Dominicana's party, I met a very nice young woman named Amy, who was my friend Rey's wife. I knew about her, but hadn't met her. I liked her right away and we became drinking buddies. All throughout our stay in Cabrera, I met her at other gatherings and we always had a lot to talk about. She was a very wise and talented woman.

Friday morning we sat in our rocking chairs and continued this daily routine. Talking about last night and about today's plans. Nuris sent us a message; she was making breakfast for us. We should come over at once (which we did). Nuris was so generous and treated all of us so well, it couldn't have been any nicer.

All our friends went beyond all expectations in their treatment of the entire group. At times we actually felt a bit guilty, because we knew all these festivities, food, music and drinks had to cost a lot of money. But none of them would allow us to pay for anything.

Arnaldo took us to another place, a small, familiar restaurant, where I was supposed to meet an older man, Rubi Bonilla, a distant cousin of mine. Before we arrived in Cabrera, I spoke with our friends and told them I would love to meet with someone who knew my father and mother. Arnaldo knows everyone in Cabrera and the countryside and he told Rubi about me. It was so, so amazing to talk to him; he remembered me as a child and so many things about my parents. I am forever grateful to Arnaldo for arranging that meeting with Rubi. After a couple of hours, we had to leave.

For our next project, we went for a drive in the countryside, where we visited two beautiful villas, just plain mansions located on hills and overlooking the sea and the surrounding farms. The owners of these villas were extremely nice to us. They offered us drinks and asked us to stay for a while, but we couldn't stay, as we had other projects awaiting us. We thanked these people and one of the owners gave us some bottles of wine. (They own a winery and produce their own wines.) They live in a very luxurious place, but at a high cost.

They need to have various securities, and a lot of guard dogs, 24/7. It is the only way that they feel safe.

From there we went to see Oscar Ramon (Oscarcito) and his wife, who were good friends of my friends. I did remember Oscar's parents from my growing up years, but not him. Well, while there, we had two roasted wild pigs (Habali). I had never tasted that meat before. It was like pork, but so much leaner, and we ate so much. Again, we all drank and danced and sweated. And again, we had live music, played by a young couple of musicians (a husband and wife who were both talented and charming). They played merengue, salsa, bachata and even Mexican music. Oscar's wife and his aunt were amazing hosts; they danced with us and kept on offering us more food, more drinks, the world.

The next morning, we had breakfast at Dona Iliria's again. Then we walked to the park, as the festivities of the 'Cabrerenos ausentes" has started. The park and streets all fill with people that return once every year to celebrate their childhood town and the people. For about an hour, cars, trucks, fire trucks, ambulances, motorcycles all drove through the calle Duarte to arrive at the meeting place. It was very emotional. They perform games, dances, music and other activities. It felt so strange to be among so many people that I didn't know, because when we grew up here, we knew everyone. But this Cabrera was all together different. At one of these activities, our friend Zoila went to play a little baseball, but she was wearing sandals and fell and hurt both of her arms.

After the accident, she sat down and didn't say anything. We didn't know how much pain she was in. (She was so brave.) At that time I was sitting a couple of chairs away, applying ice compresses to my head and face. One of the stray balls had hit me in the face, which caused a lot of pain over my face and head. So once again, I was in pain, but happy. Someone pointed out that Zoila was also hurt, and when I approached her and saw the pain in her eyes, I gave her my ice compress. When I noticed how her arm and hands were hanging in a very unnatural manner, I knew something was terribly wrong. She also knew, but didn't want to say anything. Her mom was sitting a few seats away from her and she didn't want to worry her. Migdalia and Dominicana were also there and I showed them what I saw. Migdalia's husband, Luis, is a Doctor and he came over and took a look. He decided to take her to the nearest town for x-rays. They would confirm that she had two small cracks in her bones. Dona Vida was also there with us and she was so sad. We went over to Nuris and she decided that Zoila and Dona Vida should stay and sleep over. She gave up her own bed so that our friend would be more comfortable. Zoila was in a lot of pain, so we gave her pain medication and took her to the bedroom. Nuris and I undressed her and took care of her personal necessities. After she was ready to go to bed, I left with Dominicana. I needed to go to my room to prepare for departing the next morning.

Our friends Maritza, Loa and Charo went to the park for the last night's dance. They had a great time. When I got in front of my apartment, I told Dominicana I was going to be okay. I wanted her to go home and prepare for the following day's departures. She had so much work to do. I was afraid to go to my room by myself. But I didn't want Dominicana to know how scared I was, because then I knew she wouldn't leave me alone. I went up the stairs and looked at my door, afraid to open it. I decided to turn around and sit on the stairs. It was around 11:30 PM and I was sitting there when Yova passed by. She said "What are you doing there?" I lied and said that the room was too warm and I was just waiting until it cooled down a bit. She sat there with me for a few minutes, but it was after Midnight and she also needed to go and prepare for the following day.

Around 1:30 AM, I saw the girls coming over. I was surprised, because it was the first night that Charo returned home with the girls. She had always come home later. When I saw them, I ran upstairs, opened the door and stood there to receive them. Maritza stayed down for a little while to buy something to eat. They never knew I was sitting on the stairs for over two hours.

On Sunday morning, Maritza got up earlier and got ready to leave. She was going home to Puerto Plata. We got ready to leave also. I was going to leave with Dominicana. Loa and Charo were going to stay in Cabrera for 5 more days, but at some other apartment. Charo went to stay with some relatives that she had been estranged from for years and they had a very loving time. We were all so happy for Charo, since she was able to reconnect with her relatives. For more than 20 years, there had been some family differences and they had grown apart. So this was a win-win situation.

Loa went to her family as well, to perform some repairs on a house that she owned in Cabrera. Before that, we all went to Nuris to see how Zoila was feeling. Thankfully, she was feeling so much better and she had slept well, so we were happy for her. Nuris again had breakfast prepared for us, including fresh mangoes, avocados and fresh cheese. Breakfast by Nuris was a delicious treat, each and every time.

Around 11:30 AM, Dominicana, Arnaldo, Leandro, Zoila, Dona Vida and myself left for the Capital, with a heavy heart. Only our bodies were leaving. My heart (and I am sure, all my friends' hearts) would be staying in Cabrera. Dominicana and I went to her house. I had three more days before my trip to New York. During that time, I went to visit my brother Mario, his wife Fefa and their daughters, Heidi and Liza. Their home is a happy home. Mario and Fefa still work, but their jobs are very flexible. They come home for lunch, leave work early, etc. Heidi, the elder daughter, was married and had two adorable kids. Heidi and her husband, Nelson had built a second story apartment, right above her parents' home. Everyone is happy because the grandchildren and grandparents get to see each other on a daily basis. This visit, for the first time, after many years, I felt comfortable being near my brother Mario. We had a very long talk, without being specific, about deep, profound issues. We gave each other a very good hug. I was glad to hug him. From here I went to visit a very dear friend named Mireya.

Mireya is the friend who took me and my son Julio in when I went back to DR in 1975, the year I ran away from my first husband. Remember, I always ran away, didn't trust an angry man. Mireya and I used to work together at La Manicera and the two of us, together with Miriam, Esperanza, Luz, formed an amazing and happy group. I worked for two years there and those years were some of the happiest that I had known. At the same time that I was working at this place, Tato and Rey were also there. I don't recall us hanging out or having too much contact with them, though. My life was too full of worries and other things to focus on my childhood friends then. It was the wrong time and the wrong place for me to do these things.

As always, seeing Mireya gave me a happy and sweet feeling. She was (and remains) a very special person whom I admire and respect. From there, my loyal friend Leo took me to see my dear Aunt Fresa.

Fresa and her good friend Alba (another Alba, not my godmother) had prepared a great lunch for me. Leo and I had gotten lost getting there, but when we finally arrived, it was such a good feeling. Fresa always calls me *"mi hija"* and she loves me as a daughter and I love her as a mother. Her children are my cousins, but more than that, they are my siblings. We sat and talked and stopped to eat some fine rice and beans and chuletas and salad. (She knew I loved pork.) I didn't stay long, as my friend Leo had family obligations awaiting him, so he needed to take me back home to Dominicana. That evening, I went out with my sweet Tato. His real name is Manuel Tejada, but Tato is the name we called him in childhood and I still loved that name. He came over to pick me up, but Dominicana didn't feel like going out that evening. We understood and gave her space, for at least a few hours. Tato and I went to the Zona Colonial, (Colonial City), where we met Nuris, Yova and Arnaldo. We went for a walk, talked, hugged, drank of course, and were happy as only children can be. This place was so beautiful. The city maintained the original design that the European invaders had given it, but the new structures, though much more modern, still had an antique touch. There is always live music, drinks and art, even during the evening. The lights are magical, you walk and the feeling is like you are traveling in an enchanted city.

Tato suggested we go and buy chicharron at an amazing place. (Chicharron, as well as yucca, fried sweet potatoes and more beers, of course.) We decided to go back to Dominicana's place and give her a surprise. We arrived there and she was happy to see us. We had dinner, and took more photos. It was late already, around 11:30 PM, and Arnaldo and Tato are married men. They had wives waiting at home, so they got up, went out to the elevator and left. (No one said 'adios' or good-bye, we didn't want to say this word, in either language.)

The following evening, our dear friend Yova and her husband, Baltazar, invited us to come over and have a peaceful moment, just talking and remembering a bit more. Dominicana didn't feel like going again, which was okay. This time, Leandro picked me up. At Yova's place, we sat in the back yard, where there were beautiful plants, soft lights and pleasant music, music from our childhood. Baltazar, though he didn't know us, was very happy for us, and made us feel welcome in his home.

Our little group was formed by Zoila, Arnaldo, Nuris, Leandro, Migdalia and myself. It was a very nice evening, not too warm for a change, with a beautiful bright moon illuminating us. We went home early, as the following day I was to travel back home. A couple of days before, my son Nelson had called to tell me he was arriving in Santo Domingo on the evening before my departure. So we agreed to meet for breakfast. He was staying at this very private little hotel in a very secluded area of Boca Chica. He sent me the address and instructions how to get there. It was very convenient because the place was right on my way to the airport.

I asked Leo to pick me up two hours earlier so that we could stop and see Nelson. We arrived there a half-hour earlier and I thought Nelson would be sleeping still. He had just arrived after Midnight. But, my charming son was up already, waiting for his Mom. I was so happy to see him. I adore my son, did I say that before? The three of us had an amazing breakfast. I ordered fresh papaya juice and some lime. Then I had a large, freshly caught roasted fish, with tostones. Ahhh, that was good. My son tells us that this place is his favorite for two things, the food and the seclusion.

I went back to New York, to my other family. But in my heart, I knew I would be back.

A Letter to My Grandchildren

When I started to write my memoirs, I didn't know how I would conclude them. This was no easy task, as each day we accumulate new memories. But a little bird, whose name starts with K, told me, "Why don't you end with a letter to your grandchildren?" I jumped at this suggestion. There was nothing better than having the opportunity to talk to you guys. By the time you read this letter, you will already have a very good idea about my life, my amazing life.

Yes, I had an amazing, interesting and happy life, you will say, but your *abuela* also had so much suffering, so many struggles, how could her life be anything but…

That is why I need to talk to you. You see, life is what you make of it. And a good tool to own is knowing when to let go of the past and not staying stuck to the pain or suffering or anger, because it is gone. When you are very young, you do not have control of your life, so it is what it is. But, as an adult, you have to decide to make it work for you, it is in your hands, you have the power. You have to work hard at what you want, at your dreams, at your ideals. You must learn to depend on yourself for your happiness, for your accomplishments. And *work* for it, don't just sit down and complain about life.

Do ask for help, if needed, but know and trust your sources. Ask people that you know have your best interest at heart, people that love and care about you. I could suggest your parents, siblings, etc.

Speaking of your parents, on occasion, they will have to say no to you, they will make you angry, but that is okay. (Believe me, they know best.) I know it is hard at times to believe at the moment, but you will see, eventually. At the end of the day, you have to follow your own opinions, your own path. Just be prepared to work hard, to be disciplined, and you will move ahead.

My *nieta/nieto*, the main thing in life is to be at peace with yourselves. It does not matter where, or how, just look to find that balance. I hope that you will always treat people around you with respect and dignity. I do hope that all 7 of you will love and care for one another. You all have me in common and you are all in my heart. Do not allow differences to keep you apart. You may disagree with one another sometimes, which is just fine, since each one of you is unique. But please do not turn your back on one another, do not stop communicating. Please, Dorian, Eric and Maya, always look out for each other, be a family. Justice and Juniper, please always remain the good and loving friends and sisters you are today. Noah and Lila, please always be the loving brother and sister you are today, take care of each other.

I may be around and I may not be around when you all read this letter, but believe me, even if I am not physically around, I promise to be checking on you from wherever I am. And I will be loving each one of you and protecting you.

I consider myself a happy, positive person, but my main source of happiness, my greatest pleasure in life, is when I have the chance to be around you guys. Thanks for being so good and loving to me. I am forever grateful to my sons and my daughter for giving me the gift of a lifetime – BEING AN ABUELA. I look at each

Acknowledgements

I will start with the person who encouraged and inspired me to write my memoirs, Karen Rosenberg. She gave me the courage to continue writing something that I had started about 15 years ago, but was afraid to continue. She gave me examples of other peoples' memoirs, gave me tips on developing my ideas and gave me the confidence to just write freely. Her positive attitude and love made this book possible. Also, she edited my work, and corrected the many grammatical mistakes I made. Thanks so much my dear Karen, without you, this book would have never happened. My friend, Tom McDonald, also helped with editing and formatting the text, as well as creating the book's covers and leading me to Authorhouse, the publisher that he has used with success many times. Thanks to Tom. I also want to thank all of my family, especially my children, for their support and encouragement, every time I mentioned my idea about writing this book. My two older granddaughters helped me to come up with titles. They made a list for me to choose from. Thank you, my dear girls. I thank my son Julio for his beautiful work of art that I used for the back cover page. This painting was done a long time ago as a Christmas gift to me. When I mentioned my book about my life, he told me that this painting would be appropriate. (I agree and I thank you dear *hijo*.) I thank my older son Nelson, just for always bringing a loving feeling to my heart. Thanks to Richard, my husband for his patience. When I was typing, I would ask him a thousand times about spelling of so many words. Finally, thanks to my many forever friends, for so many things. I feel that my re-encounter with all of you was the motivation to finalize my book. I wanted to talk about how it all started with you, in our lovely Cabrera. Thanks for all the love. I love each and every one of you.

The Book Out of The Fire

The little girl was, oh, so happy;
Yes that is what she said;
She somehow imagined only joy,
each morning she rose from bed.

The time was so many years ago,
in a most unsettling place;
And sadness melted into the river;
Dismissed so, on the face.

The details of the entire story
belied the child's ruse;
It's not about what you remember,
it's what you choose to use.

Along the paths you wander,
with fruit falling from the trees:
It's easier to be bruised by the sun;
It's harder to feel the breeze.

Do you recall the muted laughter?
How do the children play?
She grabbed the book out of the fire
and so she smiles today.

——*T.P. McDonald*

Printed in the United States
By Bookmasters